THE BOOK OF
CURIOUS
FACTS

JOHN MAY

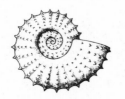

COLLINS & BROWN

The rate of exchange used in converting pounds to dollars was £1 = \$1.42. Imperial and metric measurements are given throughout, except in the case of the tonne, where near-parity with the ton makes this unnecessary.

First published in Great Britain in 1993
by Collins & Brown Limited
Letts of London House
Great Eastern Wharf
Parkgate Road
London SW11 4NQ

9 8 7 6 5 4 3 2 1

British Library Cataloguing-in-Publication Data:
A catalogue record of this book is available from the British Library.

ISBN 1 85585 043 5 (hardback)
ISBN 1 85585 201 2 (paperback)

Designed by Andy Gammon
Printed and bound in Finland by WSOY

This book is printed on Chlorine-free paper, called Munken Print, produced by the Swedish paper manufacturers Munkedal.

THE BOOK OF
CURIOUS
FACTS

'Curiosity is one of the
permanent and certain
characteristics of a vigorous
intellect.'
— *Samuel Johnson* —

TOY-MAN OF PEKIN

Believe me, believe me not!
If you believe me, it will be fine
If you do not believe me, it will rain . . .
It is not I who tells this, it is
The Old Ones who have told me this story.
— *A ritual warning with which the Malagasy tellers of tales preface their legends.*

We are still far from the time when people will understand the curious relations which exist between one fragment of nature and another, which all the same explain each other and set each other off.
— *Vincent Van Gogh*

There are, indeed, many subjects of study which seem but remotely allied to useful knowledge, and of little importance to happiness or virtue . . . yet it is dangerous to discourage well-intended labours, or innocent curiosity . . . It is impossible to determine the limits of enquiry, or to foresee what consequences a new discovery may produce.
— *Samuel Johnson*

In truth, these are but the readings of a literary vagrant. One book led to another, one study to another.
— *Robert Louis Stevenson*

Darwin delighted in snuffling through such trifles, collecting clues, the oddball, the unnoticed, the incongruous — becoming, he laughed, 'a complete millionaire in odd and curious little facts'.
— *Adrian Desmond and James Moore*

Experience has shown, and a true philosophy will always show, that a vast, perhaps the larger, portion of the truth arises from the seemingly irrelevant.
— *Edgar Allan Poe*

CONTENTS

An Introduction

This is a book about absinthe and umbrellas, menstruating men and imperial airships; about methods of towing icebergs, the restoration of limbs and species, the whereabouts of Einstein's brain, the production of vanilla, the origin of jigsaws and the history of Malagasy; about the art of demolition and electric echidnas. It is also about underground orchids, Kamikaze pilots, condoms, guide dogs and the true location of Utopia; about origami, suicides, people who have travelled round the world in unusual ways and people whose names suit their occupations; about the man behind the Great Wall of China and the origin of chewing-gum – to name but a few of the subjects you will find covered in varied depths herein.

It exists outside the confines of traditional scholarship and enquiry, a refuge for fugitive pieces of information, a place where they can breathe easily and not have to worry about their inability to fit into existing categories. We forget that all classification systems are a convenient myth designed to make us feel in control of a totally chaotic universe. Do not expect a traditional arrangement of subjects, or even an alphabetical framework. Just jump in and see what connections and meaning you can find. This book is dedicated to the disruption of set modes of thinking.

☞

Iwould like to think that *Curious Facts* is working in a long and distinguished tradition which includes such historical curious-fact collectors as:

☞ Pliny the Elder, author of the first encyclopaedia, the *Historia naturalis*, which ran to 37 volumes. Pliny spent his whole life noting down miscellaneous information about all known facts and myths and died during the eruption of Vesuvius in AD 79, while taking notes. He was collecting facts literally up to the last moment of his life.

☞ The French Encyclopaedists, led by Diderot, who produced a massive 28-volume work between 1750 and 1800, containing an enormous variety of 71,818 articles that formed both a compilation of information and a philosophical manifesto.

☞ Charles Fort (1874–1932), who spent a large part of his life poring over library archives and shuffling shoeboxes stuffed with newspaper clippings, then worked this raw data about unexplained phenomena into a new world view which he expounded in rich prose.

☞ Robert L. Ripley of *Believe It or Not!* fame, who, at the height of his popularity, was receiving up to one million letters a year. He travelled extensively in search of the curious nature of reality and once wrote: 'I make my living out of the fact that truth is stranger than fiction.'

Remember that before there were museums there were cabinets of curiosities. These could be actual pieces of furniture or whole rooms filled with odd assortments of objects gleaned from the furthest reaches of the world and arranged, to our modern eyes, in a random fashion. Gentlemen and ladies of an earlier age would take a grand tour across Europe to visit them and marvel at these rarities and relics.

The collection of John Tradescant the Elder and Younger, great gardeners of their day, formed the foundation of the

Ashmolean Museum in Oxford; and Sir Hans Sloane's collection of 79,500 objects (his house is still open to the public in London) was the basis of the British Museum.

I myself was fortunate to visit on many occasions the famous Potter's Museum of Curiosity, formerly housed in a custom-built Victorian building of strange design in the little village of Bramber in Sussex. Here, on many a winter's evening, I would gaze in wonder at the glass cases in which were contained such items as a mummy's hand, a plume from King Victor Emmanuel's hat, a dumdum bullet and a Roman horseshoe. Most impressive of all were the pair of white, wrinkled Siamese-twin piglets who stared mournfully out from their bath of formaldehyde.

Tabloid journalism also sprang from these roots. Take, for example, the magazine *Answers to Correspondents*, founded by Alfred Harmsworth in June 1888. Based on the idea that, as compulsory education had been introduced eight years earlier, this would create a whole new market of readers, it was packed with headlines like 'Can Snakes Kill Pigs' and 'The Strange Things Found in Tunnels'. It was such a success that Harmsworth applied a similar technique to newspapers by launching the *Daily Mail*.

✄

The book that you hold is the product of many years of random investigation into the nooks and crannies of the absurd and the unusual.

I have been trying to answer the question as to why I should have spent more than fifteen years of my adult life collecting a large library of books, magazines and newspaper clippings on all manner of arcane subjects, with little success. It's something to do with trying to make sense of myself and the universe by examining the little atoms of information excluded from the official model. Being by nature an outsider, this appeals to me. I am also obsessed by patterns which, as the new sciences of chaos and complexity reveal, are the basis of all that we know. And I spent a large part of my childhood with scissors and glue, reading encyclopaedias, trying to solve general-knowledge crosswords and collecting everything from bubble-gum wrappers to bits of broken china.

I have attempted several definitions over the years of my *Curious Facts* enterprise. One such is that it is a mixture of stimulating information, unusual comparisons, queer coincidences and strange stories, produced in a style lying somewhere between Barnum and Borges – showmanship and erudition.

On one level, I have sought to construct an entertainment that I hope will be read and enjoyed by people of all ages and types. On another level, this is a book about the random nature of real life, the relativity of experience, the pursuit of knowledge, the compression of information and the nature of truth.

So, dear readers, here's hoping you find some genuine inspiration, entertainment and laughter in these pages.

John May
Lewes
March 1993

IN-FLIGHT INCONVENIENCE

The American Association of Flight Attendants documented 1,172 cases of 'carry-on baggage abuse' in a single month in 1986. It lobbied the Federal Aviation Administration to introduce rules to restrict the bulk and weight of hand baggage, as the regulations for domestic flights only require that items should fit into clothes cupboards, beneath seats or in the overhead bins.

One man brought on board a 10-foot (3 metre) artificial tree which he was taking from one museum to another. An Arizona cattleman carried on the mounted head of his prize longhorn steer. Other examples of 'abuse' include a life-sized stuffed pony, a car door, a robot, ironing-boards, a slot machine, a rocking-horse, leaded glass windows, a 500-lb (225-kg) computer, the driveshaft of a BMW and two tricycles with children still riding them.

On one flight a drunk demanded his set of golf clubs should be placed in the cockpit, but there was no room as it was already occupied by another passenger's grandfather clock.

COCK & BULL

In 1990 the Taiwanese coastguards seized a Hong Kong smuggler's ship filled with 28 tonnes of rooster testicles and cow innards bound for Taiwanese dinner tables. Apparently restaurants use smuggled supplies because local testicles are more expensive.

TORONTO TROUT-TAGGING

A tag that had been attached to a Canadian trout as a publicity gimmick by the *Toronto Star* newspaper in 1937 was found on the shore of the Isle of Skye by crofter Peter McSween in 1987. *The Star* paid the $5 reward, but the question remains how the trout crossed 3,000 miles (4,825 kms) of ocean; one theory is that it did so in the belly of a larger fish.

HISTORICAL AIR

Scientists have been scouring museums across the US for objects and relics that might contain 'historical air' — air that has been trapped for decades or even centuries, without mixing with today's atmosphere. Such air would provide clues as to historical levels of carbon dioxide. Items include military brass buttons, hour glasses, antique telescopes, hollow trophies and nautical instruments that had to be sealed against salty air. Cremation urns from a Buddhist temple in Hawaii were examined but were not sealed tightly enough to be of any use.

In October 1992, samples of genuine seventeenth-century American air were obtained from inside three occupied lead coffins disinterred from a Maryland churchyard. The project cost $500,000. Scientists believe that this was a small price to pay for what could be the 'Rosetta Stone' of atmospheric science, which will enable them to decode the composition of the historical air.

Dr Steve Miller of Seattle warned readers of *Boomerang Newsletter* about boomerang elbow, thumb knuckle blisters, haematomas of the catching arm and William Tell forehead – the damage sustained when trying to knock an apple off your own head.

Playing bagpipes can cause permanent ear damage and acoustic trauma, according to two American researchers, who reported their findings in a letter to the magazine *Head and Neck Surgery* in 1988. The noise in a piper's ear can reach 115 decibels – louder than a chainsaw and just below the noise generated when a jet aircraft takes off. Bagpipers are also prone to lung infections from a fungus that grows inside the bag.

Stendhal syndrome is named after the nineteenth-century French writer who first noted the extraordinary physical reaction that results from hypersensitivity to works of art. In Florence, 107 (predominantly male) victims have been registered in the past eight years.

Amongst other medically recognized occupational or recreational ailments are: pizza-cutter's palsy, jogger's nipple, photocopier's papillitis, Space Invader's thumb, ice-hockey lung, dog-walker's elbow, yo-yoer's finger, unicycle sciatica, roller-disco neuropathy, water-ski colon, butcher's thigh.

In 1988 doctors at the Massachusetts General Hospital in Boston identified the cause of a previously unexplained medical mystery – embalmer's curse. The symptoms are loss of sex drive, impotence, shrinking testes, loss of body hair and the growth of breasts – all the hallmarks of a body producing too much oestrogen. The doctors discovered it was caused by a compound contained in embalming cream which, if used without gloves, is absorbed into the body.

Milker's head is a comprehensive fracture of the spine caused when a cow leans on your head whilst it is being milked.

The occupational hazards of musicianship include: hornplayer's hernia, violinist's neck, cellist's back, double bassist's spine, clarinettist's and oboeist's thumb, flautist's elbow and percussionist's palsy.

Hanan hand is a condition developed by Chinese cooking enthusiasts when their fingers become inflamed through contact with red chilli peppers.

Weil's disease is a sometimes fatal form of jaundice spread by contact with water or other materials contaminated by the urine of rats or other animals. Miners, farmworkers and sewer workers are the most vulnerable people, but watersports enthusiasts are also at risk.

Scrum strep is a bacterial infection passed around by rugby players; herpes gladiatorium by wrestlers. Water-skier syndrome is suffered when skiers are bounced into the water and run over by the boats towing them.

Chiropodists face a hazard from toenail dust – blown into the air by trimming drills, it may cause an allergic reaction similar to hay fever.

Mrs Pamela Osark was awarded £2,250 ($3,200) damages in October 1982 after suffering tea lady's elbow because the teapot she was forced to use at Hawker Siddley Water Engineering was too heavy.

THEFT

In January 1975, the Nairobi St John's Ambulance Brigade appealed to a thief to return a life-sized human model used for teaching artificial respiration. It was stolen, along with a suitcase, from a member of the brigade at a Nairobi bus stop.

In September 1975, a 58-year-old New York lawyer was charged with stealing more than 15,000 books from the New York Public Library. The hoard was discovered by firemen who were checking the building after a fire in another apartment. The books were piled to the ceiling and covered every available inch of floor space; they had been stolen over a period of ten years. It took 20 men three days to move them in seven truckloads. The lawyer's only comment outside the courtroom was 'I like to read.'

So many milk crates are stolen in the US – at least a million a year, worth £50 million ($71m) – that 12 Californian dairies formed a group called the Coalition for Milk Case Recovery to track them down. Unauthorized possession of a milk crate carries a £275 ($390) fine and 90 days in prison. The crates are purloined for a wide variety of inventive purposes – 1,800 were found in a market garden, full of potting compost and growing plants. In one case, CMCR investigators discovered crates were being shredded and shipped to Taiwan for recycling as toys and sewer pipes.

Three burglars broke into the office of a factory at Vang in Norway in August 1977, set dynamite to blow the safe, and went into the next room for protection. The safe was full of dynamite instead of money. As a result, one of the burglars was severely injured, the factory was badly damaged, and the thieves got just 250 kroner ($50). One of the two other burglars was arrested for drunkenness and admitted the break-in.

In a similar case, a man broke into a house in Fulham, south-west London, in March 1984 to steal copper piping, and removed it from a live gas supply. When he lit a match so as to see in the dark, the house exploded. He survived unhurt and continued stripping the central heating system while the house was on fire. The following day, when he returned to steal some more, he was arrested, and he was sentenced to four-and-a-half years' imprisonment.

In March 1984 a North Sea gas rig engineer was fined £500 ($700) with £1,500 ($2,100) costs for stealing a pocket-sized emergency transmitter from a gas rig off the Suffolk coast.

The transmitter, which the engineer had hidden on top of a wardrobe, developed a fault and began transmitting a VHF distress signal. This was picked up by a satellite and relayed to a 'foreign power', and the information passed to the RAF. An air-sea search using Sea King helicopters proved fruitless, but the signal was finally tracked to the engineer's home.

The world's shipping industry is swindled out of about £30 billion ($42.6b) a year. The IRA once swindled a Norwegian bank out of £10 million ($19.2m) by making off with a shipment of cod en route to Nigeria.

A resident of Houston was so in love with buses that he stole 100 of them – his passion was born when his mother went out with a bus driver. A court ordered him to keep away from them in future or face 10 years in prison.

A man from Essex was given a conditional discharge when he appeared before a magistrate's court in Harlow, charged with stealing 965 bus-stop signs over a 13-month period. He had finally been caught red-handed by a bus inspector while halfway up a ladder dismantling a sign. In a statement to the police, he said, 'I wanted to open a museum. I have a very great interest in public transport.' He was ordered to pay £25 ($35) costs.

QIN

Qin Shi Huangdi, the first sovereign emperor of Qin, came to power in China as a 13-year-old boy in 246 BC, and over the 15 years of his reign created

the first of China's centralized bureaucratic empires. He abolished the feudal system, codified all laws, and unified the languages, weights and measures and coinage. He was responsible for the rebuilding, expansion and unification (some say instigation) of the Great Wall, which stretched for over 3,700 miles (6,000 kms), one-twentieth of the Earth's circumference, from the Pacific Ocean to the Gobi Desert.

Never a man to do things by halves, he lived in a palace 1½ miles (2.4 kms) long by ½ mile (0.8 kms) wide, surrounded by a network of 270 smaller imperial palaces, built within a 60-mile (97-km) radius and linked by covered tunnels. Afraid of assassination, Qin slept in a different palace each night.

His tomb was even larger, and was concealed in a 150-foot (46-metre)-high man-made hill, now known as Mount Li. It remained undiscovered for 2,200 years. In 1974 workers of the Hsiang Village People's Commune were digging a well to the east of the main burial mound when they uncovered the first figures of what turned out to be a vast terracotta army, housed in a wood-lined vault 4 acres (1.6 hectares) in extent and buried under 15 feet (4.5 metres) of earth. This astonishing architectural find at the site now known as Pit One consisted of 6,000 soldiers, larger than life-size, with each face the portrait of an individual, along with 64 horse chariots.

Two years later three more vaults were uncovered nearby, further evidence of the huge standing army required to accompany Qin on his voyage after death. Pit Two contained a further 1,400 figures and Pit Three contained 73 soldiers guarding commanders in a chariot, though Pit Four was empty.

These were merely the peripheral structures around the main mausoleum, the vaults of an army that would stand eternal guard over its emperor.

Excavations on the hill have yet to begin, but it was known that, only four years after his burial, Qin's tomb was looted and his sarcophagus was probably destroyed.

UNDERGROUND ORCHID

Data from the US *Landsat D* satellite, orbiting the Earth 600 miles (970 kms) up in space, was used to locate one of Australia's rarest and most unusual flowers – the underground orchid.

First discovered by a young Australian farmer named Jack Trott in 1928, this extraordinary plant lives off the decaying stumps of a shrub called the broom honey myrtle. It is linked to the stump of the fungus, which is essential for the orchid's survival.

The orchid flowers in May and June, producing a pale pink bloom, ranging in size from 0.3–3 inches (1–8 cms) in diameter, the larger heads of which contain up to 120 small orchid flowers. The blooms never appear above ground but they do crack the surface of the soil, allowing a vanilla-like smell to escape, thus attracting insects for pollination.

Botanists at the University of Western Australia used the satellite to locate areas of undisturbed bush-land in the wheat-growing areas of western Australia, where broom honey myrtle is most often found. They then searched the ground to locate the orchids, once thought to be extinct. Fewer than 250 plants are known to survive.

TIME

The division of the hour into 60 minutes, and the minute into 60 seconds, comes from the Babylonians who used a sexagesimal (counting in sixties) system for mathematics and astronomy. They derived their numerical system from the Sumerians, who were using it as early as 3500 BC.

'Daylight saving' – summer time – was originated by William Willett (1856–1915), a London builder, who said the idea occurred to him early one summer morning when he noticed the many houses which still had their blinds down.

The first Daylight Saving Bill was introduced in 1908, and Willett devoted considerable time and money to furthering the scheme. It first became law in 1916, a year after his death, as a wartime measure to economize on fuel. During the Second World War, 'double summer time' was introduced between April and July–August, and it continued from 1941 to 1947.

The Soviet Union introduced Daylight Saving Time for the first time at midnight on 31 March 1981.

In 1992 the watch company Citizen calculated that a total of 1,750,000 hours will have been spent putting the clocks forward on the introduction of British Summer Time – the equivalent of 200 years spent in the name of daylight saving.

The BBC first introduced the time signal of six pips at 9.30 p.m. on 5 February 1924, to end a talk on the subject of British Summer Time by Frank Hope-Jones, an expert on electric clocks.

In 1949, the National Institute of Standards and Technology in Colorado built the world's first atomic clock. It measured the oscillations in ammonia of the nitrogen atom, a tetrahedral molecule that flips inside-out like an umbrella.

In 1967, the rotation of the Earth was abandoned as the basic source of time-keeping. The definition of a second has since officially been the time it takes a caesium atom to make 9,192,631,770 vibrations.

In 1991, the computer company Hewlett Packard announced they had created an atomic clock accurate to one second in 1.6 million years.

In 1982, scientists at the University of Rochester, New York, measured the briefest event ever recorded, which lasted for one thousand billionth (1/1,000,000,000,000) of a second. A twinkling of an eye would seem like an aeon in comparison.

ALCOHOL

The Royal New Zealand Navy became the last navy in the world to scrap the daily ration of rum, on 1 March 1990.

The British Royal Navy ended theirs on 3 July 1970 – Black Tot Day. The *Portsmouth Evening News* recorded that 'Sailors in ships and establishments in the area . . . said farewell to the last issue of Nelson's Blood by conducting mock funerals and wearing black armbands.'

I. Bogomolova and S. Kimaikin, from the Soviet city of Magnitogorsk, applied for a patent in 1987 for edible bottles, made of meat and bread, so that after the alcohol inside it had been drunk, the bottle could be eaten to cut down on the alcohol level in the blood. The newspaper *Sotsialisticheskaya Industriya* said that the patent had been shelved because it was too impractical.

What may have been the world's largest gin and tonic was mixed in August 1982 at West Bend, Wisconsin. The ingredients were 500 gallons (1,890 litres) of gin, a swimming pool full of tonic, four tonnes of ice and two bushels of limes. Two thousand people drank what they could, but barely made an impression; the rest was flushed down the drain.

The highest figure for alcohol levels in the human blood may be 1,220 milligrams (per 100 millilitres of blood), which is more than 15 times the British legal driving limit. This figure was revealed at the inquest on 8 March 1979 into the death by alcoholism of an inspector at Ford's Halewood plant.

In 1987, four employees in Fortnum & Mason's food hall were dismissed for allegedly drinking their way through £62,500 ($88,750) worth of the shop's fine wines and brandies, sipping them out of paper cups during their lunch hours and tea breaks.

The famous novel and film *Whisky Galore* was based on a real incident. In 1941 *The Politician*, bound for Jamaica with 264,750 bottles of whisky aboard, hit a reef off the Hebridean island of Eriskay. The islanders looted the cargo and, despite intensive official enquiries, none of it was found; most of it was drunk within a year by the island's 200 inhabitants.

The concentration of ethanol in spirits is expressed as a percentage or a proof value. 'Proof' was defined by the British as being 57.27 per cent ethanol by volume. It was operationally defined as a spirit that had the maximum concentration of water that would still allow ignition after admixture with gunpowder.

Five of the first six Americans to win the Nobel Prize for Literature – Sinclair Lewis, William Faulkner, Ernest Hemingway, John Steinbeck and Eugene O'Neill – were alcoholics.

Tequila is a special type of mescal, named after a small village in the central Mexican state of Jalisco. Only mescal from this specific region is technically tequila. Mescal is produced several hundred miles south of Tequila in Oaxaca.

Both tequila and mescal are spirits distilled from the juice of one of 200 varieties of a cactus-like plant called the agave. The cacti are harvested after ten years, the long spiky leaves being discarded to leave a pineapple-shaped core called the pina, weighing about 100 lbs (45 kgs).

Mescal pinas are then cooked in a huge wood-fired earthen oven; tequila pinas are steamed in stainless-steel vats. A murky liquid – pulque – is pressed out from the cone, and is then distilled and stored in wooden or steel barrels.

A bottle of 1784 Château Margaux worth an estimated £305,000 ($433,000) was accidentally holed by a waiter's tray at a gathering of oenophiles at the Four Seasons restaurant in New York in April 1989.

The bottle's immense value was due to the fact that it had been bought by America's third President, Thomas Jefferson, in 1787 when he was Ambassador to France, but had never been shipped to Jefferson's cellar at Monticello, Virginia. The bottle, with the initials Th.J. scratched in the glass, was only discovered in a Paris cellar in 1985.

REAL ESTATE

Previews Inc., founded in 1933, is an unusual real-estate company that specializes in selling 'hard-to-sell' property. It regularly trades in desert islands, lighthouses, convents, game reserves, airports, buffalo ranches, *palazzi* and mansions. Amongst the properties they have handled are a carbon copy of Hamlet's Elsinore Castle in New Jersey; a house in Connecticut that rotates 12 feet (3.6 metres) off the ground; a fourteenth-century castle called Schloss Ziegenberg which was remodelled by Goethe in 1747 and used by Hitler as his headquarters in 1944–5; a waterfall in Munising, Michigan; a submarine detection tower; one of the US Virgin Islands; and the residences of five American Presidents. They also sold a 400-acre (160-hectare) complex of buildings in Homesdale, Pennsylvania, owned by the Priests of the Sacred Heart, to the Himalayan International Institute of Yoga, Science and Philosophy.

Originally named the See-It-First Bureau, its customers have included the Duke and Duchess of Windsor, Dean Martin, Gerald Ford, the wife of the former Shah of Iran, Merle Haggard, Herman Wouk, Bob Dylan and Dennis Hopper.

HOUSE SMUGGLING & THEFT

On 24 November 1978, a man in Pajala, northern Sweden, was convicted of smuggling a villa from Finland into Sweden. He got the prefabricated dwelling through customs piece by piece in an attempt to avoid paying duty. Customs officials became suspicious when he crossed the border almost daily over a long period of time.

Ray Marinko returned from his holiday in Sydney in 1982 to discover that his house in the Perth suburb of Doubleview had been stolen. He said he found 'just a hole in the ground'.

In 1971, an entire house, No. 10 Jardin Street in south London, was stolen. The police believe it has 'probably now become a nice holiday home in the country or at the seaside'.

In the States 'brick rustling' is big business, since the hard clay bricks used to build America's old industrial cities are worth more than 30 pence (50 cents) each to builders in the Southern Sun Belt. Chicago loses an estimated one building a day; St Louis city authorities reckon five buildings a week are being stolen.

EXPLOSIONS

An explosion at the General Foods factory in Banbury, Oxfordshire, on 18 November 1981, which injured nine people and sent a wall of flame through the plant, was caused by a cloud of corn starch, one of the basic ingredients in custard powder. The explosion was so intense that windows were blown out and glass fragments were found buried 4 inches (10 cms) deep in a grass verge.

In January 1983 police in Cambridgeshire warned the general public about the dangers of 'exploding' tins of black treacle after three people were hit by flying lids. It appears that the treacle expanded rapidly when it came into contact with air.

In 1975 the US Consumer Product Commission estimated that 32,000 people received emergency treatment in hospitals for injuries related to exploding bottles of carbonated drinks.

Exploding office chairs have killed one person in Belgium and one in Germany, where a 66-year-old building engineer from Wuppertal in the Rhineland died after a piece of steel penetrated his eye when he began dismantling one of these chairs in his garage. Such accidents occur with adjustable chairs fitted with nitrogen gas cylinders instead of conventional springs.

Two million of these chairs are in use in Britain; the Health and Safety Executive reported in 1986 there had been only 11 incidents, three of which caused injury. By 1988 this had risen to 25 incidents and six cases of injury, including a shattered cheekbone, broken ribs and collar bones. In Germany between 1983 and 1988, there were 30 injuries and 1,000–1,200 chairs reported as faulty.

These gas-lift chairs contain a sealed two-part cylinder, filled with nitrogen under a pressure of 40 bars – about 15 times greater than a lorry tyre. When the seat is raised or lowered, gas passes from one chamber in the cylinder to another. To prevent accidents, many firms are now fitting safety clamps.

In January 1978 there were seven major explosions in US grain elevators, which killed 62 people. Between 1974 and 1978 there were 2,500 fires resulting from this type of explosion, with damage costs running at $50 million annually.

There are more than 10,000 of these giant, windowless constructions in America, in which the nation's harvest is stored. The explosions occur because of the electrostatic charge of the fine grain particles or dust, which accumulates as the grain is transferred and transported. Additional factors may be lack of venting, low humidity and possibly the presence of methane gas. Some grain elevators hold as much as 10 million bushels of grain.

Exploding television sets are commonplace in the former Soviet Union, according to a report in *Izvestia* in November 1986. More than 400 blew up in St Petersburg alone the previous year.

Scientists are still investigating the mystery as to why certain drinks 'explode' violently after being heated in a microwave.

The most likely explanation appears to be that the microwave energy penetrates the liquid and creates a 'superheated' region an inch or so below the surface. Temperatures in these hot spots can be as much as 50° F (10° C) above the normal boiling point of the liquid.

NIXON

According to Burke's *Royal Familes of the World*, Richard Nixon is the ninth cousin of Leka I, the exiled King of Albania.

HELL

Hell is a town in the Cayman Islands; and the name of a town in northern Norway.

It is also the name of an exclusive night club, run by Doriano Maltaliati, an Italian who owns six restaurants in Milan. The club, which opened at the end of 1991, is situated in the cellars of the 800-year-old Strahov monastery on a hill above Prague in the Czech Republic. The monastery's abbot, Father Opat, regards *Peklo* ('Hell' in Czech) as a useful way of raising funds for much-needed restoration work.

ORIENTATION

The word 'orientation' derives from the fact that, on medieval maps, Jerusalem was at the centre and East was at the top, where Eden, the earthly paradise, was believed to be located. The placing of north at the top of world maps has had unfortunate political and cultural consequences, reinforcing the tendency of people in the northern nations to 'look down' on the south.

DEAD LUCKY

In 1982 in San Salvador, it was reported that police believed relatives of a man who had bought a winning $40,000 lottery ticket, but had died before he'd claimed his prize, had illegally exhumed his body to search for the ticket.

In 1986 in Malaysia, a man was jailed for three months in Kuala Lumpur after he was found guilty of digging up a corpse for guidance in betting on Malaysia's weekly lottery. He said he exhumed the body, took it into the jungle to pray for winning numbers, but did not win.

In the Philippines there is a custom of playing cards while the body lies in mourning. When a law was passed banning gambling except in licensed premises, gambling operators in the Manila suburb of Mandaluyong took to borrowing corpses from hospitals for a fee in order to use them as 'props' in mock wakes.

KNUR & SPELL

Sam Ansell is the world's only officially registered referee in the game of Knur and Spell. This ancient pastime, which preceded golf, is played with a porcelain ball (the 'knur') which is hit by a stick with a wooden block on one end, from either a spring trap (the 'spell') or a 'pin' – a contraption like a miniature gallows, from which the knur is suspended in a loop or cord. Whoever strikes the knur the furthest in an agreed number of strokes is the winner. Mr Ansell, a retired clog-maker who lives in Colne, Lancashire, has to weigh each knur on a pair of tobacconists' scales to make sure it weighs half an ounce (14 gms).

OXYGEN COCKTAILS

The Ukraine Sanatorium at Yalta on the Black Sea is one of 2,000 special holiday hospitals offering a wide variety of special treatments to sick Russians with the necessary roubles. Apart from offering 'air, sun and water bathing', the Ukraine also supplies patients with 'oxygen cocktails', which sound like a delightful pick-me-up. They are made from the juice of sweet briar, vitamin C and egg-yolk. This concoction is then injected with pure oxygen and the result is a light foamy drink that is 'very tasty'.

JAPAN

Japan is a 2,000-year-old nation that consists of 3,937 islands covering 145,267 square miles (376,227 sq kms).

Japan has 200 volcanoes, of which Mount Fuji is the highest. It last erupted in 1707.

Buddhist priests at Tokyo's Kawasaki Diashi temple spend every day in a strange religious ceremony – blessing cars. Since 1963 one of the temple's parking lots has been reserved exclusively for this task, which the Japanese believe wards off misfortune. It is also a profitable business. Working an eight-hour shift, the priests last year earned $1 million for the temple, charging $10 a car and selling car safety devices on the side.

In the 1980 election, the eight national television and radio stations had, by law, to provide each of the 1,000 candidates with 30 minutes of free air-time to present their views. As a result, the nation was subjected to 6,700 political speeches, taking up some 616 hours of broadcast time.

The 1992 election campaign featured 30 minor parties including the Japanese Vinegar-Loving Party, the Invention Politics Party and the UFO Party.

Sony, the giant Japanese electronic corporation, was originally named *Tokyo Tsushin Kogyo*, but in 1953 its founder, Akio Morita, discovered, to his surprise, that the British found this hard to pronounce. Sony comes from *sonus*, meaning sound, and the expression 'sonny boy'.

The Daiichi Kangyo Ginko, one of Japan's largest banks, with more than 350 branches, has had one attempted robbery in 100 years of business.

Out of curiosity, a British businessman inspected the passageways of the Yurkucho-Ginza underground system in the centre of Tokyo, which is ten times the size of London's Piccadilly Circus underground station, for litter. In 1,200 yards of passageway he found 19 cigarette-ends, 28 matchsticks, 11 sweet-wrappers and four pieces of paper. This was during the rush hour.

The New Year season in Japan is celebrated around the country by performances of Beethoven's Ninth Symphony by professional and amateur musicians alike. In December 1987 there were 139 scheduled performances of the symphony, including one in Osaka featuring a chorus of 10,000. NHK, Japan's semi-governmental TV station, broadcasts weekly lessons at this time of year on how to sing the Ninth.

The tradition's origins are obscure. German prisoners-of-war are said to have staged the first performance in Japan in the town of Naruto during the First World War. The first known Japanese performance was at Tokyo Arts University in November 1924.

The Ninth phenomena may have evolved out of economic necessity. Orchestras needed to arrange a major concert at the end of the year in order to be able to pay their musicians the annual bonus traditional in Japan.

Japan's love of the Ninth has had wider implications. The world standard for compact discs, a maximum 72 minutes of playing time, was set in 1970, to ensure that a performance of the Ninth could fit on a single disc.

October 18 is National Statistics Day in Japan.

More than seven people are crushed into 10 square feet (1 sq metre) of space in parts of Tokyo's rail system during the rush hour, according to a survey by a Japanese insurance company. The survey also found that 15.1 per cent of Japanese have to travel for more than one hour to work, compared with six per cent of Americans and two per cent of Belgians. In Tokyo the figure increases to more than 47 per cent.

A typical office worker on a five-day working week spends a total of 18,620 hours – more than two whole years of his 38-year working life – in crowded trains.

In 1989, according to the Tokyo Metropolitan Police Department, 185,000 cars were parked on the streets of the city at any given time, and 160,000 of these were illegally parked. In 1990 there were 75.4 million vehicles on Japanese roads.

A whole new type of labour accident has now been officially recognized in Japan – 'karoshi', or death from overwork. According to government statistics, Japanese workers are on the job an average of 2,150 hours a year, compared with 1,924 hours in the US and 1,655 hours in Germany. Japanese typically use only half their allocated paid vacation time of 20 days a year.

Mitsubishi Oil has introduced a system whereby those failing to take their paid leave are fined Y1,000 (£4.23/$6) for every day they turn up at work

Some 22 billion pairs of disposable chopsticks are used in Japan annually. It is estimated that about 60 per cent are made from lumber procured outside Japan.

There are three million *burakumin* or 'untouchables' in Japanese society, the descendants of a group legally stigmatized as outcasts during the Tokugawa feudal era (1615–1867) due to their defiling jobs as tanners, butchers and gravediggers. These second-rate citizens are excluded from getting jobs in Japan's major corporations and there is no discussion of them in the media or by the government.

In 1989 Japan lost 176,000 man-days to industrial action, while Britain lost more than four million and America 17 million in the same year.

During the summer initiations for new employees and university students – known as 'Ikki, ikki' or 'Down in one!' – the pavements of Tokyo are littered with inebriates. In 1991, 9,122 people were rushed to hospital with acute alcohol poisoning, and six died.

Osaka's public transport employees receive an 'endurance allowance' of £4.20 ($6) for being punched, slapped, bitten or head-butted by drunks.

A study by two Japanese scientists discovered that their countrymen make the world's worst drunks but that the lack of one key enzyme in their bodies prevents them from becoming alcoholics. Many Japanese turn bright red when they drink, for the same reason.

A 1990 survey of Tokyo children aged between four and nine showed that one-third had their own telephones and half had their own TVs.

Two-thirds of Japanese live with aged relatives in homes one-third smaller than their British equivalents. Fewer than half of Japanese homes have main drainage. Almost 40 per cent have no flush toilets.

Housing costs in Tokyo are the highest of any metropolis. Residential land prices are 89 times higher than New York, 33 times higher than London and 23 times higher than Paris.

ICEBERGS

Seventy per cent of the world's fresh water is locked up in the Antarctic ice-cap and between 5,000 and 10,000 individual icebergs are 'carved' from this vast ice-mass every year.

The notion of making use of icebergs was first suggested in 1792 by Erasmus Darwin – the English physician, inventor and poet, and the grandfather of Charles Darwin – in his epic scientific poem 'The Economy of Vegetation', in which he suggested that icebergs should be navigated into tropical waters to reduce extremes of temperature.

Using lake and glacier ice for refrigeration dates back to Roman times, but the first case of iceberg towing occurred in the 1890s, when small bergs were towed from Laguna San Rafael in southern Chile to Valparaiso and Callao, further up the coast.

The advent of refrigeration saw the end of the trade in natural ice, but in the 1950s the idea of using icebergs as a source of fresh water was revived by John D. Isaacs of the Scripps Institution of Oceanography in California, who suggested that Californian water shortages could be alleviated by towing small Alaskan bergs south or hauling large Antarctic bergs north.

In 1973 two major studies on the subject by two teams of scientists were published. Weeks and Campbell examined the feasibility of towing icebergs from Antarctica to a coastal desert location. They analysed the costs and concluded that fresh water could be produced for a few thousandths of a cent per cubic metre, a small fraction of the cost of desalination.

An ambitious proposal, by John Hult and Neil Ostrander of the Rand Corporation, suggested lassoing icebergs with cables and arranging them into 'trains' up to 50 miles (80 kms) long. These would then be hauled by atomic-powered tugboats on an

8–10-month journey to California at the most economical towing speed of one knot. To reduce melting en route, the icebergs would be covered with special plastic 'quilts', which would restrict water loss to 10 per cent of the berg's weight.

Hult and Ostrander became so enamoured with the scheme that they resigned from Rand and set up their own company to try and develop the concept but were unable to raise the $30 million required to get the operation off the ground.

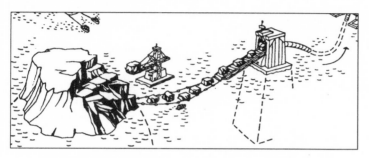

However, rapid development of the whole concept came through the interest and funding supplied by Prince Mohammed Al Faisal of Saudi Arabia, the head of the country's huge $15 billion sea-water desalination project, who saw it as a way of solving his country's critical water shortage. Icebergs looked like a cheaper alternative.

In 1977, the Prince formed a company to find a way of transporting a 100-million-tonne iceberg the 9,000 miles (14,500 kms) from Antarctica to the Red Sea port of Jiddah. He spent £1 million ($1.42m) in the first year and sponsored the First Conference on the Use of Icebergs, held at Ames, Iowa.

The Prince enlivened the proceedings by chilling the drinks with ice from a 4,785-lb (2,170-kg) 'growler' that had been plucked by helicopter from the waters off Alaska, ferried to Anchorage, packed in a huge styrofoam box, flown to Minneapolis, trucked to Ames and unloaded on the Iowa State University campus – all for a total cost of $14,000.

In 1979 anthropologist William Arens's book *The Man-Eating Myth* attacked popular conceptions on the subject and one of the great sacred cows of anthropology.

Its basic argument was simple: there is no hard evidence that cannibalism has been practised *routinely*, as a regular custom, by any tribe, in any nation, in any form, ever.

Aside from well-documented cases of 'survival' cannibalism under extreme circumstances, Arens could only find second-hand accounts and lots of hearsay. Nevertheless, almost every people on Earth stands accused of the practice at some point in history. (The term *cannibalism* was first noted by Columbus as one of the names of the warlike Canibales people of the Caribbean, who were said to eat human flesh.)

The scientific debate over this issue is far from over, with fresh discoveries only adding to the controversy. In 1986, a team of French and American archaeologists published their investigations of the 6,000-year-old remains of more than a dozen Neolithic men, women and children in a cave at Fonbregoua in south-east France. The bones were found in three shallow pits next to ten similar pits containing animal bones. The cut marks and breakage patterns on both sets of bones were identical, thus suggesting cannibalistic practices.

More recently still came the discovery of the bones of at least seven people who occupied

Gough's Cave in Cheddar Gorge in south-west England, where animal and human bones were found mixed together, again displaying identical marks and breakages. To some experts this is evidence of cannibalism; to a significant proportion of others, it signifies some kind of ritual burial practice. As Paul G. Bahn so neatly put it: 'The idea of cannibalism is, it seems, becoming increasingly hard to swallow.'

Margaret Visser in her book *The Rituals of Dinner* is of a different opinion. She says that the result of Arens's theory was to cause 'a useful flurry of research, examination, discovery and controversy. The result has been to make it clear that the sources we have cannot be discounted.'

The evidence from the Aztecs alone is proof of this. They fought wars to provide themselves with prisoners, who were eventually eaten. The estimated number of victims consumed annually at the time the Spanish arrived in Mexico in the sixteenth century ranges from 15,000 to 250,000.

Visser further quotes anthropologist Paul Shankman who examined forms of cannibal cooking practice. They included roasting, boiling, steam-baking and smoking. Human bones were often dried and powdered and subsequently used as an ingredient in sauces and juices.

The worldwide success and notoriety of the 1992 Oscar-winning movie *The Silence of the Lambs*, with its infamous cannibalistic anti-hero Dr Hannibal Lecter, found chilling substantiation in fact with the trials of Jeffrey Dahmer in Milwaukee, who confessed to killing and cooking at least 11 youths, and that of Andrei Chikatilo, a former language teacher from Rostov-on-Don, who admitted killing 55 people over a 12-year period from 1978. Chikatilo indulged in ritual cannibalism; his preference was for the sexual organs of his victims.

In 1981 Nikolai Dzhumagaliev from Alma-Ata, the capital of Kazakhstan, was jailed for murdering a string of women. He ate their flesh and even served them up to unwitting guests. He broke out of his psychiatric hospital in August 1989 and was still on the run in May 1992, our latest reference.

Equally gruesome was the 1981 case of Issei Sagawa, who killed and ate his Dutch girlfriend in Paris. Declared insane, he spent three years in a French jail before he was sent back to Japan on condition that he should be confined in a mental hospital. In fact he was discharged 15 months later and currently lives in Yokohama. His life has been celebrated in a prize-winning play and his memoirs were a bestseller. He is editing an anthology of short stories of cannibalistic fantasies and remains obsessed by his dangerous passion. In a 1991 article he confessed, 'My long-cherished desire is to be eaten by a beautiful Western woman.'

Colorado's favourite cannibal is Alferd (*sic*) Packer, a trapper and guide in the 1870s, who killed and ate his five travelling companions when they ran out of food in the mountains. Packer was convicted of cannibalism, and the judge who sentenced him in 1874 is reputed to have said: 'There was only six Democrats in all of Hinsdale County and you, you man-eating son of a bitch, ate five of them. I sentence you to hang till you're dead, dead, dead, as a warning against further reducing the Democratic population of this County.' In fact Alferd was paroled after serving 16 years and lived to a grand old age.

In July 1982 a bust of him was permanently installed at the restaurant of the University of Colorado in Boulder, which was renamed the Alferd E. Packer Memorial Grill. A plaque to Alferd's memory had also been unveiled in the grill room of the Agriculture Department in Washington, DC in 1977 but was taken down after the General Services Administration complained that: 'This reflects badly on the meals that are served to Government employees in Government restaurants.'

In January 1990, the *Independent* reported that Swaziland would be deporting Hitler Sharin, a self-styled mercenary and self-confessed Moroccan cannibal, because he had been demanding the bodies of road accident victims for his meals.

COLOUR

Isaac Newton named seven colours in the spectrum – red, orange, yellow, green, blue, indigo, violet. You can't really see indigo as a separate colour, and orange is doubtful, but Newton added them because he liked the number seven.

According to his biographer, Newton 'had a penchant for crimson – crimson draperies, a crimson mohair bed with crimson curtains, crimson hangings, a crimson settee'.

Richard Wagner liked to have some violet in his surroundings when composing operas. The musical note associated with violet is B.

Rubens, Renoir, Dufy and Klee used much bolder colours than their contemporaries and suffered from rheumatic diseases as a result. All were slowly poisoning themselves, according to modern-day research conducted in Copenhagen and reported in *The Lancet*.

The first three used bright red paint (containing mercury and cadmium), bright yellow (containing arsenic, cadmium and lead) and blue (containing copper and cobalt, contaminated with arsenic, aluminium and manganese). All had rheumatoid arthritis. Klee, who used bright red and violet, suffered from scleroderma, a disease that hardens and wastes the skin.

It has been suggested that Van Gogh's obsession with the colour yellow ('How beautiful is yellow') may have come from his taking digitalis, a common remedy at the time for a wide range of maladies, including epilepsy. This is known to produce visual disturbances and abnormalities of colour vision. The foxglove, from which digitalis is derived, is portrayed in Van Gogh's portrait of Dr Gachet of Auvers.

The discovery of the colour mauve laid the basis for the modern-day chemical industry. An 18-year-old chemistry student named William Perkin discovered it by accident in 1856 when he was trying to synthesize the drug quinine at his London home. Instead he produced mauve, the first synthetic dye.

The dye turned out literally to be worth its weight in gold, as Perkin discovered that it was particularly effective at permanently colouring silk. The 1890s became known as the Mauve Decade, so fashionable did it become.

Perkin subsequently set up a number of dye factories, grew very rich, was knighted by Edward VII in 1906 and retired to continue studying pure chemistry at the age of 37.

Paper is white because it is coated with innumerable small crystals of titanium dioxide, which throw the light back and so make the surface look white. The more crystals, the richer the white. Interestingly enough, the white powder comes from the black ilemnite stone found in iron mines. Titanium dioxide is also used to make toothpaste brilliant white, to give cigar ash an even grey colour, to make plastic opaque and to make colours in paint deeper and brighter.

In the Philippines what we call 'blue' pornography is called 'green'.

Colour pollution is a buzz-word used by landscape architects to refer to the ill-considered use of colours on buildings. The problem is the result of the explosion of synthetic colours produced by the chemical industry. More than three million colours have been synthesized and 9,000 are currently in production. Paint companies are now working with cities across Europe to develop 'coherent colour palettes' for their buildings, based on local traditions. The most extensive scheme of this kind is in Turin in Italy. Here, over the last ten years, the owners of 10,000 buildings in the city have agreed to follow the approved colour scheme; in exchange they receive a paint subsidy from the city government.

Anthropologists and linguists have discovered that human languages can be ranked according to how many terms for colour they use.

Two of the New Guinea Highlands languages use only two colour terms – one that covers white and all the light hues, another that covers black and all the dark ones. The next rank includes Pomo, the language of the Native Americans of California, which has names for only white, black and red.

After this come languages that include first green, then yellow, followed by blue and brown; then, in no fixed order, purple, orange, pink and grey. The maximum number of basic colour terms seems to be 11.

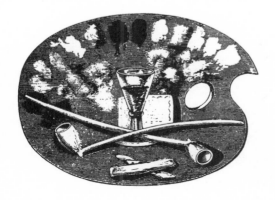

In ancient Egypt dinner guests wore cones of scented fat on their heads which melted 'deliciously' as the meal wore on.

On 31 December 1853, a dinner party was held inside Mr B. Waterhouse Hawkins's lifesize model of a prehistoric iguanodon, built for the newly created primordial swamp at the Sydenham Crystal Palace on the outskirts of London. Invitations were sent out 'on the wing of a pterodactyl' to 21 eminent scientists, who ate and drank their fill and sang songs like 'The jolly old beast/ Is not deceased,/ There's life in him again.' A report in the *Illustrated London News* records: 'After several appropriate toasts, the agreeable party of philosophers returned to London by rail, evidently well pleased with the modern hospitality of the Iguanodon, whose ancient sides there is no reason to suppose had ever before been shaken with philosophical mirth.'

In August 1992, Tokyo's Shin Takanawa Prince Hotel staged a Dinosaur Buffet to coincide with an exhibition of dinosaur fossils in another part of the hotel.

The menu included such items as Brontosaurus burgers and Stegosaurus sausages but the highlight was the 100-million-year-old dinosaur egg, a culinary concoction that measures one foot (0.3 metres) across and can feed 40 people.

The egg's creator Shizuo Inoue used pumpkin for the egg yolk and a mixture of spinach and minced chicken for the albumen. The

shell was made of ostrich eggshell, which was pasted on the outside before cooking. Three hours of steaming were required before it was ready to eat. It was served with dinosaur-shaped bread.

In February 1868, a horsemeat banquet for 160 was held at London's Langham Hotel. The highlight of the meal was a 280-lb (127-kg) baron of horse carried on the shoulders of four chefs, which gourmets decided tasted like roebuck. The motto of the occasion was 'Prejudices are afflictions of the human spirit'.

A 'horseback dinner' was given in the grand ballroom of the fashionable Sherry's restaurant on 28 March 1903 by C.K.G. Billings, who was heir to a Chicago gas fortune and mad about horses. To celebrate the opening of his $200,000 stables in the city he invited 36 guests, each of whom was supplied with a horse. The saddle carried a dining tray, and there was champagne in the saddle-bags, which was drunk through rubber tubes. The waiters were dressed as grooms.

PI

Pi is the ratio of a circle's circumference to its diameter, expressed approximately as 3.142 but more precisely to an indefinite number of decimal places. By the end of the sixteenth century pi was known to 30 decimal places, and the calculation has been extended ever since.

In 1987, pi was computed to more than 100 million decimal places (2^{27}). Thirty-nine decimal places are sufficient to calculate the circumference of a circle around the known universe with an error no greater than the radius of a hydrogen atom.

HOT DOGS

The term 'hot dog' was coined by cartoonist Tad Dorgan in 1901. He worked in the press box at the old polo grounds in New York, and one day he drew a cartoon of Harry M. Stevens, who sold 'dachshund sausages' on rolls. He termed them 'hot dogs' because he couldn't spell 'dachshund'. Stevens's company is now one of the biggest hot dog concessionaires at US sport stadiums.

PTOLEMY'S CRIME

Ptolemy, the Greek astronomer whose theory of an Earth-centred solar system held sway for 1,400 years until the time of Copernicus, was a scientific fraud, according to Dr Robert Newton in his book *The Crime of Claudius Ptolemy* (1977). Ptolemy claimed that his ideas were derived from observation, but in fact it appears that he simply worked backwards from the answer he wanted and that his observations are far too precise to have been made with the simple astronomical instruments of the period. It appears he also stole figures he needed from another astronomer, Hipparchus, and then changed them all by the same amount to get the results he wanted and claimed the new observations as his own.

SEAGULL-SHIFTER

In 1986 Frank Murray, a professional steeplejack, began work in Arbroath as Scotland's first official seagull remover. The gulls first became a menace after being attracted to the town in large numbers by the easy feeding from a local fish-processing works.

TOILETS

The first wall-hung men's urinal was designed in 1908 for the Larkin Building in Buffalo.

The Human Lavatory was a medieval public servant who walked the streets in an immense cape, which he used to cover his customers and the pail he carried, according to a history of the lavatory by Colin Lucas.

Failure to flush the loo in Singapore's public lavatories will earn you a £48 ($68) fine for a first offence, a £163 ($230) fine for a repeat offence, rising to £326 ($460) for persistent offenders.

Reuters reported in October 1985 that Vaduz, the capital of Liechtenstein, was holding a referendum to end a three-year wrangle over where a public toilet should be built.

Japan's largest maker of toilets, TOTO, has introduced the Washlet, a cross between a toilet and a bidet. It has a heated seat, sprays your derrière with warm water and dries it with a blast of warm air. Added attractions on the more expensive models are a built-in deodorizer, and a hand-held wireless remote control to activate front and back sprinklers. According to a spokesman for the Japan Toilet Association (Motto: 'Clean, fresh, I am toilet'), the country uses enough toilet paper every day to circle the Earth ten times. In November 1986 it sponsored Public Toilet Day, with panel discussions and lectures, one of which was devoted to the idea that 'Toilets should be sunny places.'

The shortest reign by a Pope was that of Stephen II, who was elected on 23 March 752, and died the following day. As he was never consecrated, his name was omitted from the Vatican records and given to his successor.

Forty Popes have died within a year of taking office. The quickest turnover was between April 896 and December 897, when there were no fewer than six Popes.

The longest-serving Pope was Pius IX, who was elected in 1846 at the age of 54 and reigned for 32 years.

The oldest Pope was the 80-year-old Adrian I, who was elected in 772 and lived to be 103. The youngest Pope was Benedict XI, elected at the age of 12 as a political intrigue against two 'anti-Popes'; he was reaffirmed in office twice and died at the age of 25.

Twenty-six Popes have been murdered, 13 jailed or exiled.

When a Pope dies, the papal secretary has to call out his original Christian name three times before he is officially declared dead. His 'Fisherman's Ring', given to him at his coronation, is broken, as is the papal seal, used for documents of state. In the nineteenth century the papal secretary also had to tap the dead Pope's head with a silver hammer.

The cardinals who elect the Pope can be found guilty of their own special crime – simony, or selling their votes for money or power. In 1272, the cardinals took two years and nine months to make up their minds. In exasperation, angry Catholics sealed them up in a room until they came to a decision – a practice that has continued ever since. The shortest election on record was in 1939; it took them just one day to decide on Pius XII. (It was rumoured that Hitler had sent a spy to infiltrate the election.) One of the 115 cardinals who are eligible to vote will succeed as Pope. An unsuccessful outcome – an inconclusive ballot, which fails to reach a majority of 75 votes (two-thirds plus one) – will be signalled to the world by black smoke from the burnt ballot papers; a successful one by white, chemicals being added to ensure a clear signal.

On 5 November 1982 a handful of ticker-tape brought the Pope's bulletproof vehicle – the Popemobile – to a halt in Granada, Spain. It had filtered through the engine grill and caught fire, forcing the Pope to transfer to a bus full of bishops.

Pope John VIII was poisoned in 882 but his poisoners couldn't wait and finished him off with clubs. Pope John X was poisoned by his mistress's lunatic daughter. Celestine V was poisoned by Boniface VIII. Benedict XI died after someone put powdered glass in his figs. Paul II died after eating melon. There are grounds for believing that Mussolini had Pius XI killed by Dr Petacci, the father of the Duce's mistress. Pius XII died from hiccups.

The church tailors Slabbinck of Bruges, who generate a £2 million ($2.8m) turnover supplying churchmen all over the world with vestments, spent 100 hours working on a bishop's hat for Pope John Paul's tour of Belgium in May 1985 – only to discover it was the wrong size.

Pope Clement was thrown into the sea with an anchor round his neck. Calixtus was clubbed and thrown down a well. Lucius II was killed by a brick.

Stephen was decapitated on the papal throne. Leo V was burned and hurled into the Tiber.

John XXI was killed when his palace collapsed on him. Pelagius XI died of a plague which induced terminal sneezing.

Legend has it that, at the very moment of Pope Fabian's election in AD 236, a dove landed on his head.

The Pope rules over the Vatican State, a principality of just over 100 acres (40 hectares), with a maximum length of 1,132 yards (1,035 metres) and a maximum width of 812 yards (742 metres). It has 400 citizens, the majority being members of the Pope's armed forces, the Swiss Guard. It has its own flag, radio and railway stations, fire department and heliport. It mints coins and prints stamps. There are no taxes. It has its own TV station, pharmacy and newspaper – the *Osservatore Romano* – which has a daily circulation in Italy of 100,000 and a weekly international edition.

STATUES

An unusual story is attached to the equestrian statue of King William of Orange, which used to stand on College Green in Dublin until it was blown up by the Republicans in 1929. The remains of the now headless statue were dumped in a junkyard and forgotten until the Second World War when Dublin's water supplies were under threat. Thousands of gallons were being lost every day, owing to leaks from ancient piping, and lead for repairs was scarce. It was then that an engineer noticed that King William's horse was exceptionally well endowed and that its private parts – which weighed a stone and a half (9.5 kgs) – were made of solid lead. The problem was solved. Embarrassed council officials kept the matter secret for decades.

N.T. Rama Rao, an eccentric Indian film star who had spent his career playing gods and megalomaniacs, became Chief Minister of the central Indian state of Andhra Pradesh and proceeded to lavish 65 million rupees ($3.2m) on building a 350-tonne granite Buddha – said to be one of the world's biggest monoliths.

Most of the cost was taken up by transporting it 35 miles (56 kms) from Raigiri to Hyderabad, where it was to be placed on an island in the middle of a lake. A special hydraulic trailer with 24 axles and 194 wheels had to be built, and a huge jack was imported.

In 1990, three-and-a-half years after the project had begun, the 500-tonne rock was loaded on a giant construction barge to carry it the few hundred yards to the island.

Within minutes disaster struck. The barge began to tilt, the Buddha rolled into the lake, and the 40 people on board jumped for their lives. Eight of them died.

During the 1950s the largest Stalin statue in Europe, 100 feet (30 metres) high, brooded over Prague. In the early 1960s, the city authorities blew it up. After the fall of the socialist governments in 1989, Stalin memorabilia became attractive to collectors in the West, and a hunt was instituted for Stalin's head. All that could be found was a button – the size of a large loaf of bread.

When Australian Neil Glasser was given the task of finding a statue of Queen Victoria to front one of Sydney's best-known landmarks, the restored Queen Victoria building, he discovered there were a total of 126 statues of the late queen worldwide. He eventually discovered the one he wanted in the town of Daingean, 60 miles (96.5 kms) west of Dublin, and transported it to Australia.

The orchestra did not play *Nearer My God to Thee* as the *Titanic* went down – a fallacy fostered by the two feature films, *Titanic* and *A Night to Remember* – but an episcopal hymn called *Autumn*. As one survivor, Lawrence Beesley, wrote in a letter in 1962, 'The band is not likely to have suggested to those on board that presently they would be in the presence of their Maker, quite apart from the fact that as the deck was on a slope of 45 degrees or more, they could not stand to use their instruments.'

Nor did millionaire Jacob Astor quip, 'I ordered ice but this is ridiculous.'

The model of the *Titanic*, built for Sir Lew Grade's film version of Clive Cussler's best-selling book *Raise the Titanic*, cost £3 million ($4.2m) – half a million more than the original ship cost to build. Only when the hull was completed was it realized that a new £2 million ($2.8m) artificial tank would have to be built to sink her in, as none of the existing ones were big enough. The movie lost £10 million ($14.2m) and almost sank Grade's Associated Communications Corporation. He is reported to have quipped, 'It would have been cheaper to lower the Atlantic.'

In 1992 there were 12 remaining survivors of the *Titanic* believed to be still alive. Three of these were women living in Britain. Seven hundred and three people survived the disaster; either 1,517 or 1,521 people drowned, but no one is sure exactly.

RADIO MAN

One lesser known aspect of the *Titanic* tragedy occurred on 14 April 1912, when the young radio operator and manager of a five-kilowatt radio station, the most powerful commercial station then operating, picked up a faint message from the SS *Olympic*, 1,400 miles (2,250 kms) away. When deciphered through the static, it read, 'SS *Titanic* ran into iceberg. Sinking fast.'

For the next three days and nights, with all other radio stations closed down by presidential order, the operator stayed glued to his earphones in New York, waiting for the names of survivors as they were hauled from the ocean.

He wrote years later: 'Much of the time, I sat there with nothing coming in. It seemed that the whole anxious world was attached by my earphones during the seventy-two hours I crouched tensely in the station.

'I felt my responsibility keenly, and weary though I was, could not have slept. At the end of this, my tryst with the sea, I was whisked in a taxi cab to the old Astor House on lower Broadway and given a Turkish rub. Then I was rushed in another taxi cab to Sea Gate, where communication was being kept up with the *Carpathia*, the vessel which brought in the *Titanic* survivors.

'Here again I sat for hours – listening. Now we began to get the names of some of those who were known to have gone down. This was worse than the other list had been – heartbreaking in its finality, a death-knell to hope. I passed the information on to a sorrowing world, and when messages ceased to come in, fell down like a log at my place and slept the clock round.'

The young man in question was David Sarnoff, founder of RCA.

CHEIRO

Born on 1 November 1866, the son of Count William de Hamon and Mademoiselle Dumas, 'Cheiro' became the most successful palmist of the age, and the most flamboyant. He had undoubted skill in spite of the fact that, as Fred Gettings puts it, 'his theory was unsound, his knowledge of the history of the subject ludicrously inaccurate, his sense of honesty sadly impaired, and his sense of importance verging on megalomania'.

Cheiro's life story is suitably improbable. He claimed to have studied palmistry in India under Brahman Joshi Cast and when aged 28 published his first book, *Language of the Hand,* which sold 5,000 copies in four months. He was a press correspondent during the Russian-Chinese wars, ran a champagne business under another name, worked as a scriptwriter in Hollywood, became a Fellow of the Royal Geographical Society and claimed to have saved a young anarchist from the firing squad by hypnotizing the boy and duping the executioners with blank ammunition. He wrote novels and plays and his book *World Prediction* was a bestseller. He predicted the exact date of death of Queen Victoria, Edward VII and Lord Kitchener, and claimed the latter was a case of murder.

56

Tea caused the destruction of ancient China (to pay the high cost of tea, the East India Company tried to sell opium to China, which led to the Opium War of 1839–42), sparked off the American War of Independence (the Boston Tea Party), led to the introduction of porcelain into Europe, had a dramatic effect on the economy of India, and permanently influenced ship design.

For nearly 200 years all Britain's tea came from Canton, on China's southern coast. Tea was unknown in India except as an import.

The Canton-Macao name for tea was *cha*, corrupted to 'char'. The British upper classes, the only ones who could afford it, called it 'tay', spelled 'thé'.

Demand outstripped supply and, as a result, tea was adulterated with twigs, wood, pine bark, alien leaves, sawdust, soot and Prussian blue. Bergamot, the flavouring that gives Earl Grey its distinctive taste, was first added as an adulteration.

Porcelain was shipped from China with tea as saleable ballast. Between 1684 and 1791, the East India Company shipped an estimated 215 million pieces. In 1730, a tea service for 200 people cost seven guineas.

The Chinese made tea in kettles. The teapot, inspired by the Chinese wine flask, was a European invention, as were teacups with handles.

The first known discovery of a wild tea plant in India was in 1820. The Assam tea industry was founded in 1860; those of Ceylon and Java in 1890.

GUILLOTINE

Dr Joseph-Ignace Guillotin (1738–1812) introduced this method of execution into France in 1792. Known in French slang as *la veuve* – the widow – the shape of its triangular blade (the 66-lb/30-kg 'sheep') was suggested by Louis XVI, who was later to lose his head by this method.

Guillotin only claimed credit for the 'simple mechanism' of this device, which had been first designed by Dr Antoine Louis in 1789, and saw the linking of his name to it as an attempt to embarrass him politically. A moderate member of the Revolutionary Convention, he escaped being guillotined himself only by volunteering for war service in a military hospital.

Ironically, the guillotine was conceived by the revolutionaries as a humane instrument to replace the existing methods of execution, whereby criminals had their bones broken and were then pulled apart on a wheel.

Madame Tussaud's famous waxworks were founded largely to expose the horrors of the French Revolution. She acquired the blade of the original guillotine in 1854 along with drawings that were used to reconstruct an accurate model of the whole scaffold. A copy of this full-scale model was rebuilt in the 1960s.

The last person to be executed by guillotine in France was Hamida Djandoubi, a 28-year-old one-legged Tunisian, found guilty of torturing and strangling a young woman, at Baumettes Prison, Marseilles in 1977. The death penalty was abolished in France in 1981.

MALLEE FOWL

The mallee fowl (*Peipoa ocellata*) is one of 13 species of megapode (large-footed) mound-building birds, most of which are confined to the Australasian region. They use the heat of fermenting vegetable matter to incubate their eggs, building mounds of decaying leaves and rubbish, which they then cover in sand.

Although male and female birds generally pair for life, they each lead a solitary existence, meeting only rarely. The eggs are very large, one-tenth of the female's body weight, and are laid singly; they take between five and ten days to produce. On average a female will lay 19 eggs each year but may lay as many as 33.

These are carefully covered and uncovered by the male over a $5^1/_2$-month-long period, during which time he strives to maintain an even temperature in the mound.

When each baby chick hatches it takes between two and 15 hours to struggle unaided from the mound; once it has emerged, it leaves the nesting site and rarely, if ever, sees its parents. By the second day it can fly.

In 1990 the scrub fowl (*Megapodius reinwardt*) was implicated in an archaeological controversy over whether large midden-like mounds, found along the northern coast of Australia, are created by generations of these birds, by aborigines, or by a combination of both.

BURIALS

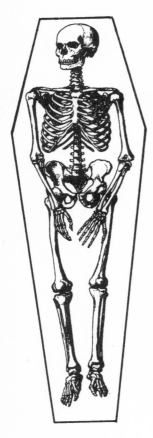

In 1977 the owner of a cemetery in Livingston, Montana, was sentenced to dig graves by hand after he was convicted of hiding bodies instead of burying them. Police found 30 unburied corpses in a mausoleum at the Park View Cemetery.

There is a Society for Perpendicular Interment in Melbourne, Australia, which believes that people should be buried upright in cylindrical cardboard coffins.

Major Peter Labilliere, an eccentric eighteenth-century gentleman who lived in Surrey, left instructions in his will that his landlady's son and daughter should dance on his coffin and that he should subsequently be buried head-down vertically on Box Hill. A stone still marks the spot.

There are no civil or religious impediments to vertical burials, it seems, but there are practical and aesthetic considerations, as Bill White pointed out in response to a question in the *Guardian's* Notes and Queries. He wrote: 'Unless expertly and expensively embalmed, a dead body will disintegrate. While remaining undisturbed in a horizontal attitude the component bones will approximate to the human form. However, a vertically buried cadaver under gravity would deposit a jumble of disarticulated bones that might be regarded as unacceptable.'

This objection to vertical burial was cunningly overcome in a 1977 patent application by Alfred Schmitz of Oregon, who proposed a plastic coffin with three internal projections that support the body under the armpits and the groin. A spring-loaded valve allows the release of gases and fluids produced by decomposition.

The Kyocera Corporation, a Japanese manufacturer

of high-technology ceramics, has instituted the ultimate in corporate togetherness – the company tomb. Employees can join their late colleagues in a sepulchre at a Zen Buddhist temple situated between Kyoto and Osaka. Inscribed on it are the following words: 'We pray that the souls of the deceased will go peacefully to the Other Side . . . sometimes getting together as they have in this world to talk, inspire each other and exchange cups of sake.'

Tibetans practise a ritual known as sky burial, where the bodies of the dead are fed to vultures. Bodies wrapped in white sheeting are taken by the undertakers to a large rock where they are dismembered and cut up, the bones pounded into fragments and mixed with barley meal. The chief undertaker then calls down the vultures, holy birds in Tibetan tradition, to feed on the remains. In their Buddhist tradition, everything must have a purpose. Therefore, once the spirit has left the body, it must be used to feed the birds. This is also a practical method of corpse disposal in a land where there are very few trees for burning bodies and the ground is frozen solid for most of the year.

Stephen Charles-Davis, a former osteopath, runs the Britannia Shipping Company for Burial at Sea, headquartered in Newton Poppleford, Devon. For £654 ($925) you can be buried in a coffin or a traditional shroud and the firm guarantees that all materials used are non-toxic and biodegradable. Every burial requires a special licence from the Ministry of Agriculture, Fisheries and Food, which also specifies an exact location for the burial, to avoid it getting trawled or dredged up by fishermen.

In the US, the nation's largest sea burial conglomerate is called the Neptune Society and is owned and run by Charles Denning, who has earned the nickname 'Colonel Cinders'.

Bongo is the unlikely name of a Warsaw-based organization that makes a living out of the dead, shipping 500–600 bodies of Polish émigrés back to the motherland for burial each year.

In March 1986 Reuters reported that undertakers in Bonn had mistakenly buried a one-legged tramp in a millionaire's coffin, while the rightful occupant lay on a mortuary slab for a week.

In 1981 Stanley Zelazny and Michael O'Piela of Kansas patented a solar-powered talking tombstone, which contains a tape machine with a recorded message from the dear departed.

The ultimate burial scheme was that devised by a syndicate of Florida morticians, Celestis Group Inc., working in collaboration with former astronaut Deke Slayton's company, Space Services Inc. of Houston: cremated ashes or even freeze-dried, vacuum-packed corpses were to be sent into orbit.

The first flight, scheduled for 1986, was to have contained the ashes of 8–12,000 corpses, each reduced to the size of an Oxo cube and sealed individually in a monogrammed gold-plated capsule, at a cost per head of £6,000 ($8,500). The idea never got off the ground.

The environmental effects of corpse disposal are only just beginning to be recognized. According to two Swiss environmental consultants, in a paper published in *Nature* in 1991, the average human corpse emits as much as a $1^3/_4$ lbs (1 gm) of mercury vapour and a smaller amount of lead vapour when it is cremated. The former may come from the evaporation of amalgam dental fillings; the origin of the latter is unknown. The implications of these findings are that a modern city crematorium working at full capacity emits 22–28 lbs (10–13 kgs) of mercury a year.

In a related story, it was revealed that the typical adult embalmed male contains almost 21 pints (12 litres) of formaldehyde, a known carcinogen. What residents of Hamilton, Ontario were worried about in January 1991, when they raised objections to the building of a new cemetery in the area, was that it would leak out and contaminate the ground water. It appears that embalmed corpses could be considered a form of toxic waste.

Among the displays in a 1975 exhibition called *London As It Might Have Been* – a collection of plans of buildings for the nation's capital that were never built – was a scheme for a giant pyramidal mausoleum to be constructed on Primrose Hill.

The idea came from one Thomas Wilson, who, in 1824, was concerned about the acute problem of finding space to bury the dead. His solution was a pyramid large enough to contain five million corpses, stored in 215,296 catacombs, each with 24 coffins, which would occupy only 18$^1/_2$ acres (7.5 hectares) of ground. Made of brickwork faced with granite, it had a base as large as Russell Square, was considerably higher than St Paul's Cathedral, and had a huge flight of stairs on every side. A central shaft would have facilitated interment, and the whole giant structure, 94 storeys high, was to have had an astronomical observatory on top – all for a total cost of £2.5 million ($3.5m).

Wilson commented: 'The grand Mausoleum will go far towards completing the glory of London! It will rise in solemn majesty over its lofty towers to proclaim by its elevation the temporary triumph but final overthrow of Death – teaching the living to die and the dying to live forever.'

BIKINI

The precise connection between the US nuclear test above the Bikini Island lagoon on 1 July 1946 and the invention of the two-piece swimsuit has never been established – but there are many versions of the story.

Designed by Frenchman Louis Reard, an engineer by profession, the first bikini was cotton and printed with a newspaper design. It was revealed at a Paris fashion show on 5 July 1946, and modelled by the dancer Micheline Bernardi.

As for the name, Reard coined the word to express his concept of the 'ultimate', according to one version. The Parisian evening paper *France Soir* asked its readers to guess how the name originated. One suggested that its wearer looked as if she had just emerged from a bomb blast. Certainly Reard had created a different kind of 'bombshell' that was to gain almost as many headlines as its thermo-nuclear namesake. The shock of the bomb and the shock of the bare midriff appeared to be roughly equivalent.

Louis Reard died, aged 87, at Lausanne in Switzerland on 17 September 1984.

INK-SLINGERS

The following are names of newspapers published in the Wild West:

Kansas Prairie Dog, Cheyenne County Rustler, Clark County Clipper, Cash City Cashier, Morganville News and Sunflower, The Saturday Cyclone, The Brick, The Eye, The Allison Breeze and Times, The Head Centre and Daily Morning Sun, The Broad Axe, Grip, Locomotive, Kansas Cowboy, The Ryansville Boomer, Hill City Lively Times, Western Cyclone, Conductor Punch, Cimarron Herald and Kansas Sod House, The Montezuma Chief, Ensign Razzoop, Border Ruffian, The Jayhawker and

Palladium, Santa Fe Trail, Comanche Chief and Kiowa
Chief, Daily Infant Wonder, The Scout, Gopher and
Winona, The Hatchet, The Fanatic, The Comet, The
Boomerang, The Hornet, The Wasp, Astonisher and
Paralyzer, Inkslinger's Advertiser, Grisby City Scorcher,
Sunday Growler, The Prairie Owl, Springfield Soap Box, The
Whim-Wham, Sherman County Dark Horse, The Bazoo,
Thomas County Cat and Grit.

KNOTS

There are about 4,000 kinds of knot, which can be
broken down into many different families and
groups.

The British Association of Knot Tiers includes
amongst its membership a man from the Isle of
Wight who ties knots inside bottles.

Former police inspector Geoffrey Budworth, a knot-
ting consultant to the National Maritime Museum,
claims that it is possible to spot the personality
behind a knot, and his manual on the subject, co-
written with forensic scientist Dr Sheila Keating, is
used by police throughout Britain.
 Knots can reveal the sex, job and hobbies of a
person and, sometimes, whether they are left-handed.
In one murder case a knotted cord used to strangle a
victim was identified by Budworth as an angler's
knot. The killer was a keen fisherman.

WAVES

One of the great sea mysteries of the twentieth century, the disappearance of the *Waratah* in 1909 off South Africa between Durban and Cape Town on her second voyage, with 119 crew and 92 passengers on board, may be explained by a chance encounter with a 'freak' wave.

There is growing evidence that such giant waves, which can exceed 100 feet (30 metres) in height, should in fact be termed 'episodic', since there is an underlying logic to their formation. They tend to occur in particular locations, usually on the edge of the continental shelf, and under particular conditions of current and weather. To this extent, the places and times of year at which they can be expected are predictable.

The dangers that they pose to shipping have increased in recent years with the growing number of enormous flat-bottomed transport vessels, such as giant oil tankers. Whereas traditional 'ship-shaped' ships, with sharp bows and deep keels, tend to cleave through waves, bulbous-nosed, barge-like tankers rise up on giant crests and then slam down into troughs. The results are frequently catastrophic – ships bent and buckled, or even broken apart.

Freak waves, episodic or otherwise, can also pose a threat to people and property on the shore. In 1977, 50 people were swept from a breakwater on the Channel Island of Alderney by a 60-foot (18-metre) wave.

At the beginning of this century Captain D.D. Gaillard of the US Army Corps of Engineers devoted his career to studying the forces of such waves on engineering structures. His 1904 report includes the following examples:

• At Cherbourg in France, storm waves hurled stones weighing 7,000 lbs (3,175 kgs) over a large rock breakwater capped with a 20-foot (6-metre)

66

high wall, and moved concrete blocks weighing 65 tonnes some 60 feet (18 metres).

• At the Tillamook Rock Light, off the Oregon coast, a heavy steel grating protects the lighthouse beacon, which is 139 feet (42 metres) above low water. On one occasion, a 135-lb (61-kg) rock was thrown above the lighthouse keeper's house, the floor of which is 91 feet (28 metres) above water, and fell back through the roof, wrecking the interior.

• In 1872, the designer of a breakwater at Wick, Scotland, which was capped with an 800-tonne block of concrete secured to the foundation by iron rods over 3 inches (7.6 cms) in diameter, watched in amazement from a nearby cliff as the whole thing, weighing 1,300 tonnes, was removed by a wave and dumped into the water. He subsequently rebuilt it, adding a larger and heavier cap weighing 2,600 tonnes. This received similar treatment during a storm a few years later. Gaillard computed that the force of the waves must have been 6,340 lbs per square foot.

ABSINTHE

The liquorice-tasting liquor absinthe was concocted principally of alcohol and the bitter-tasting herb wormwood – so bitter that one ounce (28 gms) can be detected in 524 gallons (2,380 litres) of water. It was flavoured with extracts from a variety of herbal plants, which variously included anise, fennel, badi-ane, hyssop, melissa (lemon balm), juniper, nutmeg and others according to regional taste.

Absinthe was reputedly invented by Pierre Ordinaire, a French doctor living on the Swiss side of the border with France. When he died, his house-keeper inherited both the recipe and one of her best customers: Major Henri Dubied manufactured the drink on a larger scale with his son-in-law, Henry-Louis Pernod, and a dynasty was founded.

The initial enthusiastic consumers of this toxic beverage were French soldiers, who had developed a taste for wine spiked with wormwood extract during the Algerian conflicts of the 1840s. The habit soon spread to the artistic community and *l'heure verte* (the green hour) became an established daily event. Its effects have been immortalized and portrayed in works by Manet, Degas, Toulouse-Lautrec, Daumier, Baudelaire, Verlaine, Rimbaud, Jarry, Apollinaire and many others.

Toulouse-Lautrec reportedly roamed Montmartre carrying absinthe in the top of his hollow cane, his favourite tipple being a mixture of this and cognac, a drink nicknamed *tremblement de terre* (earthquake).

Van Gogh was almost certainly addicted to absinthe. When he died, his doctor planted a thuja or white maple tree on his grave – an ironic gesture, since the tree is a principal source of *thujone*, the toxic principle of absinthe, which exacerbates psychosis and causes hallucinations.

Between 1875 and 1913 the annual consumption of absinthe per head in France increased 15-fold and in 1913 alone 10.5 million gallons (48m litres) were consumed. In and around Arles, consumption was four times the national average. Medical knowledge of the drink's deleterious effects accumulated, leading to a formal prohibition on its sale and manufacture in France in 1915.

Today the only legal way to obtain a bottle of absinthe is by purchasing one of the original Pernod bottles through an auction house.

UMBRELLAS

Umbrellas – parasols and parapluies – were first invented by the ancient Chinese or Egyptians, or both, some 3,000 years ago and were considered a symbol of royalty in places like Burma and Assyria. They spread into northern Europe from the Mediterranean regions (the name derives from *umbra*, the Italian word for shade) but were considered primarily a French feminine accessory during the seventeenth and eighteenth centuries.

In England owning one of these predominantly silk parasols was thought to be effeminate and degrading, indicating that you were unable to afford a carriage. The pioneer of umbrella usage was the Victorian reformer and founder of the Marine Society, Jonas Hanway, widely credited as the first man to venture through the streets of London carrying one. He suffered the abuse of coachmen and sedan-chair carriers, whose trade improved when it rained, and was even stoned and whipped by them.

His umbrella was not only handsome but collapsible. Apparently, 'the handle was ebony and all covered with small fruits and flowers. The outside was pale-green silk, and the inside was stone-coloured satin. When opened, it was like a small tent, and when shut it was all curiously jointed and would fold up to the length of a man's hand.'

In 1850 Samuel Fox of Stockdale patented steel ribs, which replaced whalebone; and this, coinciding with the import of Tonkin cane from Indochina, provided the basis for the stronger and lighter umbrella that became *de rigueur* during the Victorian and Edwardian eras.

Tests conducted in 1990 in wind tunnels at the College of Aeronautics at Cranfield, Bedfordshire, and using a range of umbrellas, indicated that none could cope with a wind speed of more than 32 mph (50 km/h) without blowing inside-out.

CHESS

The Mongol emperor Tamerlane played Great Chess on a 110-square board. New pieces introduced included a princess (combining the moves of bishop and knight), an empress (rook and knight), and an amazon (queen and knight).

There are 400 different possible positions after each player has made one move; 71,852 after the second; more than 9,000,000 after the third. According to George Steiner, the number of distinct, non-repeating 40-move chess games that can be played is much greater than the estimated number of electrons in our universe.

Wladyslaw Glinski is the Polish inventor of hexagonal chess, which features a board of 91 hexagons of three colours, instead of the standard 64 black and white squares, and one extra pawn and bishop. First conceived when he was a schoolboy, the game was finally brought to the marketplace by Glinski nearly 50 years later, in 1985.

Humphrey Bogart was a chess hustler on Broadway and later in Hollywood. The scene in which Rick plays solitaire chess in *Casablanca* was his idea.

The most astonishing collection of ancient chessmen in existence comprises the 78 pieces – seven or more incomplete sets – discovered on the island of Lewis in the Outer Hebrides in the spring of 1831. A storm had undermined a sandbank on the west side of the island to reveal a small stone building, inside which the chess figures, carved of morse ivory (walrus tusk), were preserved. The detailed nature of the costumes of these figures has allowed experts to date them to c.1170, and it is believed they were carved in Iceland or Scandinavia.

COMPUTER CHESS

The idea of a machine that can play chess dates back to the 1760s, when an automaton, nicknamed the Turk, was exhibited in Europe. It beat Napoleon Bonaparte in 19 moves, but its secret – a diminutive chess master hidden in a secret compartment – was later guessed by Edgar Allan Poe.

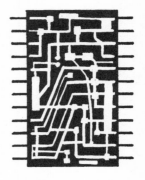

Twentieth-century computer pioneers, mathematicians and game theorists like Alan Turing, Claude Shannon, John von Neumann and Oskar Morgenstern, all analysed the game, but it was not until 1958 that it was possible to program a computer to observe the rules of chess. In 1966 *Machack-6* became the first computer to reach the standard of an average tournament player, and in 1974 a computer program Chess 4.0 surpassed expert level.

Purpose-built chess machines were first designed in the 1970s, and the most famous of these – Belle – achieved chess master status in 1983. Two brute-force machines – *Cray Blitz* and *Hitech* – fought for supremacy later in the 1980s. They were able to search 100,000 and 120,000 positions per second respectively.

The current computer chess champ is *Deep Thought*. Its heart is a circuit board the size of a large pizza, which contains 250 chips, including two processors that can search 500,000 positions per second. By mid-1990 it had won five out of ten games played under tournament conditions against grand masters and had an 86 per cent score in 14 games against international masters. Its planned successor will shrink *Deep Thought*'s computing power to a single chip and link 1,000 of these in parallel, allowing it to analyse a billion positions per second.

(*Deep Thought* is named after the machine in Douglas Adam's *Hitchhiker's Guide to the Galaxy*, which pondered for 7.5 million years before announcing that the answer to life, the universe and everything is 42.)

BENDS & THE BROOKLYN BRIDGE

Divers working at depth often suffer from a crippling condition known as caisson disease, or 'the bends', as they surface. It is caused because the water pressure outside the body forces the nitrogen in the diver's blood into solution in the blood and gristle. When he rises to an area of lesser pressure, the nitrogen begins to froth; the same principle is in operation when a bottle of champagne is opened. This causes severe pain and cramps at the very least, and can clog the veins and cause death at worst.

The first medical observations of this condition were made on the 'sandhogs' – immigrant labourers – who dug the foundations for the two towers of the Brooklyn Bridge by hand. Large *caissons*, wooden boxes without bottoms, were sunk to the river bed and pumped full of compressed air to keep them watertight. The workers entered through an airlock, often emerging later to the surface crippled with pain, contorted in positions that reminded their workmates of either a popular posture fad or a ballroom dance of the time known as the 'Grecian bend'. The name stuck. Many died, their legs 'twisted like plaited hair'. Nor were the workers on the bridge the only ones to suffer. Colonel Washington A. Roebling, son of the man who conceived and designed the bridge, was permanently invalided after spending too long in a *caisson* when a fire broke out in 1871.

In 1873, aware that the bends were made worse by increasing depth, Roebling declared that the *caissons* should go no deeper, despite the fact that the bedrock had not been reached. To this day the foundations of the bridge rest on compressed sand.

72

The unlikely link between these two historical characters is the frontier governor and author Lew Wallace,
the man who saved Washington from capture during
the Civil War and presided at the trial of Lincoln's
assassins. He got religion and the governorship of
New Mexico at around the same time. The Lincoln
County War was raging by day; by night it provided
fuel for his writing, in purple ink in bound note-
books, of the story of *Ben-Hur*.

Billy the Kid, who, it was said, had killed
21 men by the age of 21, sent Wallace a letter
and a meeting was arranged for 17 March
1879, at the home of John B. Wilson. A
deal was struck. The Kid would give eye-
witness testimony on a killing in Lincoln;
in return the Governor promised Billy
he'd go 'Scot free with a pardon in
your pocket for all your misdeeds'.
Billy turned out to be something of a
'supergrass' to the Grand Jury, fur-
nishing Wallace with the 'names and
misdeeds of numerous bad men'.
Here versions differ: some claim
the pardon didn't arrive, others that
Billy lost faith and rode away.
Either way, the relentless Pat
Garrett was soon on his trail. The
rest is history.

Richard Lawrence, the first person ever to attempt to take the life of an American President, claimed that he was a reincarnation of Richard III of England. When he attacked President Andrew Jackson on 30 January 1835, both his guns misfired at point-blank range.

The young anarchist Leon Czolgosz (pronounced 'Cholgosh') shot President McKinley on 6 September 1901, while he was visiting the Pan-American Exposition. Czolgosz was badly beaten by soldiers, sentenced without a trial (he refused to speak to anyone), and executed (by electrocution) on 29 October 1901. After his death his coffin was filled with sulphuric acid so that his body dissolved. McKinley died after eight days in intensive care, singing a hymn.

Only one British Prime Minister has been assassinated in office. Spencer Perceval was shot in the lower part of the left breast at close quarters by John Bellingham, on Monday 11 May 1812, as he was leaving the House of Commons. Bellingham (41) pleaded not guilty at his one-day trial at the Old Bailey. The court was told that he had been arrested for debt while on a business trip to St Petersburg, and felt aggrieved that the British Government had not done more to extricate him. In his defence he claimed that he bore no personal malice towards Perceval. He was found guilty and hanged at Newgate and his body was delivered for dissection.

The event was foreseen in a dream. Mining engineer and banker John Williams told his vision to many of his friends, including the writer John Abercrombie, and his experience was described in *The Times* five days after the murder took place.

Among Ronald Reagan's achievements are the fact that he successfully survived the Zero Factor. Previously every President elected in the last year of any of the 20-year intervals from 1840 onwards, died in office.

There were three attempts on the life of Queen Victoria between 1840 and 1842 – one when she was fired on by a hump-backed lunatic named Bean, who escaped in the ensuing mêlée. Before he was finally caught, police were rounding up every hunch-back in London. The other would-be assassins were a potboy named Edward Oxford in June 1840 and an unemployed man named John Francis in May 1842. Bean and Oxford were judged insane; Francis was transported for life.

In May 1849 an Irish bricklayer named Hamilton fired a pistol at Victoria's coach and was sentenced to seven years' transportation, as was Robert Pate, who a year later struck the Queen on the head with a stick.

The Kennedy assassination is not the only such event to be surrounded with rumours of cover-ups and conspiracies. There are at least two persistent theories surrounding the shooting of Lincoln on 14 April 1865. The first is that it was the culmination of an elaborate covert operation by the Confederate Secret Service; the second is that the man shot in a burning barn 12 days after the assassination was not John Wilkes Booth but a farmhand, and that Booth actually died in Enid, Oklahoma, in 1903.

Incidentally, Abraham Lincoln's eldest son, Robert Todd Lincoln, was on the scene of *three* pres-idential assassinations: those of his father, and of Presidents Garfield and McKinley.

The famous Reading Room of the British Museum was initiated by Antonio Panizzi, a former Italian revolutionary, who oversaw the design and construction and extracted an annual grant of £10,000 ($14,200) from the government. He also devised the cataloguing and shelving system, the desks and the book rests.

The new British Library is currently being constructed in what is Europe's largest building development. Architects for the project were appointed in 1962 but the first earth was not turned until 1984 and the first phase (expected to cost £150–200 million/$210–285m) will not be completed until the year 2000. The architect, Colin St John 'Sandy' Wilson was 40 when he started the job and it has so far taken 27 years. The completed building, on a $9^1/_2$-acre (3.8-hectare) site by St Pancras Station in London, will have two million square feet (185,000 sq metres) of floor space, twice the size of Harrods.

Lenin's British Museum Reading Room ticket was finally found in the archives in 1990, filed under Oulianoff, the French transcription of his original name, Vladimir Ulyanov. He was first recommended for a ticket by John Teppett, an author of socialist pamphlets, but this was rejected, and Lenin had to find a new proposer – Harry Quelch, editor of *The Social Democrat*. His seat number was L13 and his choice of reading matter included the first Russian translation of *Das Kapital,* which Marx, a former user of the library, had personally presented.

The world's largest collection of periodicals available for loan is located at the British Library Document Supply Centre at Boston Spa in Yorkshire. It contains more than 200,000 titles of serial publications and subscribes to 56,000 journals. In addition there are four million books. The whole fills 100 miles (160 kms) of shelf space on the site of an old ordnance factory. In 1986 a grant of £1.5 million ($2.1m) was given to convert an old corn store to provide a further 26 miles (42 kms) of shelving. Books and magazines arrive at the rate of 4 miles (6.5 kms) of shelving per year. The Centre gets 2,800 requests on average every day.

The oldest library in Britain is in Leadhill, one of Scotland's highest villages, situated 1,000 feet (300 metres) up in the Lowther Hills. The Leadhill Miners' Reading Society was founded in 1741 and the library was instituted by Allan Ramsay, an Edinburgh bookseller who was born in the village in 1686. It is still open to visitors today and a readership card can be obtained, but the books are for reference only.

The Library of the Humanities Research Center, Austin, Texas, houses nine million literary manuscripts in a seven-storey rectangular limestone building. When it was being built in the 1960s, the rumour was that it was going to house John F. Kennedy's brain, kept alive artificially, on the fifth floor. Its holdings include the writing desks of Arthur Conan Doyle, Edgar Allan Poe and Evelyn Waugh, Gertrude Stein's skull-cap and fan, Houdini's magical equipment, the world's first photograph, Einstein's notes for the theory of relativity, Rudyard Kipling's egg cup, G.B. Shaw's walking suit, Conan Doyle's spectacles, Walt Whitman's cigar box and a collection of hair that once belonged to Samuel Johnson and which includes locks from Milton, Keats, Shelley, Coleridge and Wordsworth.

The library's manuscripts include those of *Waiting for Godot, Under Milk Wood, A Passage to India, Women in Love* and *The Seven Pillars of Wisdom* (which Lawrence lost and the University found) and an unpublished Graham Greene novel.

The University of Texas is the richest university in the world. It was the brainchild and creation of one man, the late Chancellor of the University, Harry Ransom, an ambitious anglophile with unlimited funds who began in 1972 to establish *the* library of the twentieth century.

In 1989 a Norwegian-based group of architects, Snohetta, beat 524 entries from 70 countries to win a competition set by the Egyptian Government and backed by UNESCO to 're-create' the ancient Alexandrian library. The design is described as 'a cylinder pointing to the sun and the moon', symbolizing the library's rebirth.

No trace remains of the Mouseion of Alexandria, which was founded in the third century BC, and contained the library as well as a zoo, laboratories and observatories. For 400 years it was 'the most learned spot' on Earth, a centre of Greek and Jewish culture. Its exact fate is uncertain, but it is believed that the main library was destroyed in AD 215 and a secondary building in AD 391. It is said that when the Arabs took over the city in AD 642 the public baths were heated for six months by burning books.

Inspired by Richard Brautigan's novel *The Abortion: An Historical Romance 1966*, Todd Lockwood founded a library in Burlington, Vermont in April 1990, exclusively for unpublished books. Lockwood calls its contents 'folk literature' and says, 'We are challenging the publishing industry concept that if something is not publishable, it is not readable.' Backed by friends, local authors, businessmen, writers and celebrities, he raised $10,000 to buy a binding machine and rent office space. 'The Brautigan Library. A Very Public Library' received 15 volumes in the first month. Writers must submit a synopsis of the work and a $25 fee to cover library costs; the library binds the book and puts it on the shelves.

The blind librarian of the medieval monastic library in Umberto Eco's *The Name of the Rose* was the blind Jorge of Burgos. Jorge Luis Borges, the blind Argentinian writer, was director of his country's national library. He wrote a story called 'The Library of Babel' in which 'an indefinite, perhaps an infinite, number of hexagonal galleries' held every possible combination of the letters of the alphabet and therefore the sum of all possible knowledge.

This idea was also explored by the German writer Kurd Lasswitz in his short story, 'The Universal Library' (1901), which concluded that the story itself should be regarded as 'an excerpt from one of the superfluous volumes of the Universal Library'.

George Gamow's 'One, Two, Three . . . Infinity' estimated the size of such a library and described the construction of a printing press to produce the volumes.

MAZES & LABYRINTHS

The 'City of Troy' turf maze near Brandsby, North Yorkshire, is one of Britain's four surviving turf mazes. It is based on a Cretan design, the oldest labyrinth pattern in the world, examples of which can be found on every continent except Australasia.

London's Science Museum covers a maze built by Prince Albert.

At Lappa Valley Railway, Cornwall, there is a maze shaped like Trevithick's 1804 locomotive, the forerunner of Stephenson's *Rocket*.

The maze in the Rectory Gardens at Wyck Rissington, Gloucestershire, was made by the parish priest, Canon Harry Cheales, in 1950, after being given exact instructions in a dream. (As a young man Gustav Holst was the organist at the Church of St Laurence next door.) The guide to the maze reads: 'Our life is a journey: the feet and yards of the path are the months and years of human life. The wrong turnings are the sins and mistakes we make. The path leads through life to death, then through the garden of Paradise, to Heaven.' The 'centre' is marked by a massive Wellingtonia pine, a species

which grows to 375 feet (114 metres) high and is known to live for 4,000 years. This tree was one of the first of its species to be introduced into Britain.

Randoll Coate, a former diplomat turned maze-builder, claims that even if a maze has been destroyed centuries before it can still be traced by a diviner. He has designed a maze in the form of a giant footprint, 156 feet (48 metres) long, incorporating 120 symbols in the shapes of the path, representing the two sexes, the Trinity, the four elements, the five senses, more than 20 British animals and birds and the shape of Icarus, the son of Daedalus, the designer of the Cretan labyrinth that imprisoned the Minotaur.

He has designed an egg-shaped maze for Baroness Falkenberg in Sweden, a maze inspired by a dream that the Archbishop of Canterbury had, and the only pyramidal maze in the world, in the grounds of the Prince de Ligne's gardens at Beloeil, the Versailles of Belgium.

Sculptor Michael Ayrton became entranced and obsessed with the legend of Daedalus.

In 1967 he designed and built for the New York financier Armand G. Erpf a labyrinth of 1,680 feet (510 metres) of brick and stone pathways and walls enclosing two centres, containing bronzes of the Minotaur and Daedalus.

Ayrton believed that 'the inextricable yards of intertwining intestine that man first revealed when he inserted his flint knife into his victim' gave humans their first obsession with the labyrinth. From these same mysterious internal regions, babies are connected to their mother by a cord.

James Joyce, who called his *alter ego* Stephen Dedalus, made a labyrinth that he called *Ulysses* and another called *Finnegans Wake*.

Daedalus emerged from his Cretan labyrinth on wings of his own design; Ayrton reminds us that history's first airborne invasion, in 1941, led to the capture of Crete.

An analysis by Gunter Nobis of 375 bones found in the Oxen Room of the Cretan Labyrinth at Knossos has thrown new light on the legend of the Minotaur. The bones, discovered in 1894 by the British archae-ologist Sir Arthur Evans, have proved to be those of three kinds of bull – the domestic ox, the huge but now-extinct auroch, and a cross between the two – leading Nobis to suggest that ancient Crete was a centre for bull-breeding. The mythical Minotaur – half bull and half man – may have represented the ultimate in breed.

The labyrinth may also relate to the convolutions of the brain. Angus Fletcher concludes that 'The experience of the labyrinth is that of thought experiencing itself.'

The *R100* and *R101* airships were designed to inaugurate the new Imperial air mail service to India. There was a political debate as to whether these giant craft should be built by the state or by private enterprise; in the event, the minority Labour government, under Ramsay MacDonald, decided that the *R100* would be built by the private sector, to a design by Barnes Wallis, and the *R101* by the state. The latter ended up costing the taxpayer £2 million ($2.8m), comparable to the modern cost of Concorde.

The *R100* which, by contrast, cost £363,000 ($515,000), flew to Montreal and back in 1930 in 79 hours at an average speed of 55 mph (88.5 km/h).

The *R101* was 777 feet (240 metres) long (three times the length of a jumbo jet), 132 feet (40 metres) high and contained 5.5 million cubic feet (155,650 cu metres) of hydrogen.

The giant airship was on its maiden flight to India when it crashed and burst into flames near Beauvais in northern France, killing 48 of the 54 people on board.

The airship was modified halfway through its trials and left for India before it had completed the 150 hours of flight needed for an airworthiness certificate. The government waived the rules despite complaints from the crew about its lack of stability. Lord Thomson, the Secretary of State for Air and the driving force behind both airships, pronounced it 'as safe as a house except for the millionth chance'. He died in the crash, and is buried along with the other victims in a common grave facing the airship hangars at Cardington in Bedfordshire.

(After the failure of this state enterprise, the *R100* was scrapped for political reasons. It was broken into pieces, a steamroller was run over them and the remains were sold for £450/$650).

Computer analysis conducted by Sir Peter Masefield, an air historian and former aviation chief, and Alan Simpson, a retired professor of aeronautics at Bristol University, may have solved the mystery of the *R101*'s crash.

Masefield and Simpson believe pilot error was the cause of the tragedy. (The crew throttled back the engines instead of going for height, which might have saved the cumbersome craft.) They reached this conclusion after taking all the known data into the computer and tracking the airship's progress at five-second intervals. This task, Peter Johnson reports, 'involved tens of thousands of calculations, the permutations produced by relating twelve "fixed points" – known data such as heights of ship and hill, speed, engine power – to 27 "variables", such as changing weather.'

π IN THE SKY

The familiar cigar shape of the pre-Second World War airships was formed by a series of massive rings, up to 130 feet (40 metres) in diameter, joined by girders. Each ring was reinforced and stressed by thousands of wires running to the centre. The stresses on each wire had to be calculated. The rings were different sizes, so the calculations for each had to be done separately. This was in the days before computers.

Nevil Shute Norway, best known as author of *A Town Like Alice* and *On The Beach,* worked as chief calculator on the successful *R100* airship, designed by Barnes Wallis. The calculation for just one ring took two to three months. At the end, the relief was enormous.

He described the experience in his autobiography *Slide Rule*: 'It produced a satisfaction almost amounting to a religious experience . . . It struck me at the time that those who built the great arches of English cathedrals in medieval times must have known something of our mathematics and perhaps passed through the same experience.'

WAR & PEACE

November 11th is traditionally remembered as the anniversary of the armistice of 1918 in the form of Remembrance Sunday (UK) and Veterans' Day (USA). However, in 1981 the same date was chosen for another formal armistice signing, between a small village in southern Spain and Denmark, thus officially ending 172 years of hostilities. It appears that the Council of Huescar was so infuriated by Denmark's decision to side with France against Britain in the Napoleonic Wars that in 1809 it declared war, though Denmark did not discover this fact until recently.

In April 1986 another forgotten war, that between the Netherlands and the Scilly Isles, was also officially ended. It dated back to 1651 when Dutch Admiral Maarten Tromp declared war on the islands because the inhabitants had engaging in piracy during the English Civil War.

ELECTRIC ECHIDNAS

Echidnas, also called spiny anteaters *(Tachyglossus aculeatus)*, have electro-receptors in their snouts which, researchers believe, are used to detect electrical signals given off by worms and ants. Echidnas always have a runny nose, the nasal secretions providing an electrically conductive medium that can carry tiny currents.

Platypuses, the only other surviving monotremes, or egg-laying mammals, also have electro-receptors in their rubbery bills. Some fish, including sharks, have this 'sixth sense', and it is possible that moles do as well.

84

The hairs on the thumb of the right hand grow to the left, the hairs on the fingers of that hand to the right. On the left hand, the hairs on the thumb grow to the right, on the fingers to the left. This observation comes from Dr Morris Leider of New York, an expert at painlessly removing rings stuck on fingers.

The proper anatomical names for the digits of the hand are polex (thumb), demonstratorius (first finger), impudicus (middle), annularis (ring) and auricularis (little finger).

Between 1972 and 1986 more than 60 patients in California who had lost their thumbs had them replaced by surgeons, who amputated their big toes and transplanted them. The main disadvantage of this treatment is that they then had to be given artificial big toes, otherwise walking and balance become difficult.

In 1982 police in Japan exposed a gruesome insurance swindle in which people had been cutting off their index fingers in order to collect disability payments for the 'accident' from insurance firms, usually on policies that had only been taken out a few weeks before. In August it was reported that 18 fingerless people were in custody but that 60 more were still at large. Insurance losses were estimated to total 300 million yen ($2.4m).

In 1961, the Museum of Modern Art in New York hung *Le Bateau* by Henri Matisse upside-down for 47 days before discovering their mistake.

Newcastle's 13-day biennial of innovative visual arts, *The Edge 90*, featured, amongst others:

• Mark Thompson, an artist and beekeeper from San Francisco, whose pièce de résistance was set in a disused warehouse. Its windows were bricked up with translucent beeswax bricks and in the centre was a man's skeleton on a bed, its ribcage providing space for a beehive.

• Marina Abramovic from Yugoslavia, a performance artist who sat inside a ring of ice, while pythons slithered over her.

• Guillaume Bijl from Belgium, who explored 'merchandise fetish' through precise reproductions of a market stall, a car showroom, a travel agency and a shoe shop.

One of the most cryptic sculptures ever produced is that commissioned from Jim Sanborn from Washington, DC for the entrance courtyard of the CIA's headquarters at Langley, Virginia.

The granite and copper ensemble contains a coded message perforated on a 10-foot (3-metre) copper plate supported by a petrified tree. The message – a 2,000-character phrase written by a spy novelist – is inscribed using two codes; one was invented in 1586 by Blaise de Vigenere, a French diplomat, the other by an unidentified cryptographer. Only President Bush and the Director of the CIA know what it says, apart from the two responsible for its realization, presumably.

US taxpayers unknowingly contributed $250,000 from the government's public art budget to fund the project, which the public will never see.

Stelious Arcadiou, or 'Stelarc', stages events that he calls 'obsolete body suspensions'. He puts 18 large fishhooks through his skin, attaches wires to the hooks and hangs nude from trees, cranes or ceilings for half an hour or more. Stelarc believes these events symbolize the 'physical and psychological limitations of the body' and provide his audiences with 'the visual symbol of man overcoming the force of gravity'.

In 1981, an American artist became the first artist in the history of the US to be found guilty of committing a libel with a painting. The artwork in question showed three men with face-like masks attacking a partially-clothed woman in an alley. Two fellow-artists claimed the mask faces on two of the men were clearly their own, and that the painting portrayed them as either violent criminals or artists intent on murdering art.

The court found in their favour and the artist was ordered to pay each man $30,000.

In 1978 the Art Corporation of America Inc. created a coast-to-coast conceptual art piece by hanging a banner reading LIFE from the Golden Gate Bridge in San Francisco and another reading ART from the Verrazano Bridge in New York. An airline pilot, flying between the two cities, was informed by telegram that he was carrying an invisible 'conceptual hyphen' to complete the slogan.

Performance artist Chris Burden has allowed himself to be shot, crawled barefoot through a field of broken glass, shut himself in a student locker for five days.

He once offered art gallery visitors in southern California the opportunity to murder him, after wiring his body into an electrical outlet and placing a bucket of water nearby.

Cold Dark Matter: An Exploded View was the title of a 1991 exhibition at a London gallery by Cornelia Parker, an artist fascinated by the processes of destruction. The installation involved blowing up a garden shed containing tools, suitcases full of household junk, a bicycle and a pram, to produce mutilated fragments of material. These were then arranged around a large 500-watt lightbulb suspended from the ceiling of the gallery provoking, in the words of one reviewer, 'a quiet, slightly eerie meditation on a destructive act'. The installation could also be said to refer to the Big Bang. Cold Dark Matter is the scientific term for unfathomable outer space.

Impressionist paintings look the way they do because most of the painters suffered from one or more eye defects, according to Richard Kendall.

Kendall is a leading authority on Degas and discovered that he was completely blind in his right eye by the time he was 35. In his other eye he suffered from severe myopia (short-sightedness), photophobia (the inability to stand bright light), irregular astigmatism (due to scarring of the cornea) and a 'blind spot' where he could see nothing at all.

Kendall also discovered that: Monet had cataracts for the last 20 years of his life; Cézanne was a diabetic, a condition that often affects eyesight; Renoir was severely short-sighted, as was the American painter Whistler.

Pissarro developed an eye infection in the 1890s, which meant that his eyes had to be bandaged for a long period, and Mary Cassatt went completely blind at the end of her life.

The exception to the rule was Edouard Manet, who had excellent eyesight, as evidenced by the clarity and precision of his painting.

Both Renoir and Degas were prescribed glasses but they threw them away. Renoir claimed that the glasses made him see too clearly.

Famous newspaper hoaxes range from Edgar Allan Poe's fictitious account of the first balloon crossing of the Atlantic in the *New York Sun* to the *Sunday Times*'s Hitler Diary fiasco.

Less well-known is the hoax dreamed up by James Gordon Bennett, Jr, publisher and editor of the *New York Herald*, a man who insisted on creating news as well as reporting it. In 1873, he sent Stanley in search of Livingstone to gain a spectacular media coup. Perhaps he was bored the next year. Whatever the reason, on 9 November 1874, his readers were faced with these astonishing headlines:

AWFUL CALAMITY
Wild Animals Broken Loose from Central Park

TERRIBLE SCENES OF MUTILATION
A Shocking Sabbath Carnival of Death

SAVAGE BRUTES AT LARGE
Awful Combats Between the Beasts and the Citizens

PROCLAMATION BY THE MAYOR
Governor Dix Shoots the Bengal Tiger in the Street

The graphic story was packed with incident and eye-witness accounts: how a rampaging rhino met its end in an Eleventh Avenue sewer excavation; how a tiger rampaged around a North River ferryboat.

The report read: 'Writing even at a late hour, without full details of the terrors of the evening and night, and with a necessarily incomplete list of the killed and mutilated, we may pause for a moment in the widespread sorrow of the hour to cast a hasty glance over what will be felt as a great calamity for many years.'

It was all pure fiction. The paper never apologized, except to report the following day that the fantasy had disturbed 'the equilibrium of the public' and to ask: what if the beasts had been real?

VACQUEROS

Cowboy culture began with *vacqueros,* professional cattlemen who had acquired their skills from the Spanish ranchers. They lived hard and lonely lives on the *mesas,* living in lean-to shelters of sticks and rawhide, eating jack rabbit and wild turkey.

When in town they drank pulque, made from the agave plant. They were addicted to this so much that they invented a Goddess of Pulque, who had 400 rabbit children. Drunkenness was measured on a 'rabbit scale'. A man who was ten rabbits overboard was barely high; if he reached 200 rabbits he was spectacularly drunk.

SINGING SANDS

'Singing sands' are a known scientific phenomenon existing at 30 sites around the world. When loosely settled sands are disturbed by the wind, humans or some other force, the millions of sand grains shifting and sliding over each other can create a shearing effect which causes 'singing'. Three US sites where this occurs are: Kelso Dunes in southern California, Sand Mountain east of Reno, Nevada, and Crescent Dune near Tonopah, also in Nevada.

PUNCH & JUDY

Every May Day the Punch and Judy 'professors' attend a thanksgiving service at St Paul's Church, Covent Garden. Samuel Pepys noted in his diary the first appearance of a Punch and Judy show in the church's portico.

The stock characters owe their origin to Greek mime and to the *commedia dell 'arte*, the Italian comic theatre of the seventeenth century. Punch aside, they are: Judy (called Joan until 1818), the Baby, Joey, Clown, the Policeman or Beadle, the Ghost, the Hangman, the Crocodile and, of course, Toby, who was traditionally a live dog. The Crocodile was originally the Devil, and became the Russian Bear for a short period during the Crimean War.

Punch himself developed from a stock *commedia* character – Pulcinella, a comic servant. In England this became Punchinello, which was subsequently abbreviated.

FURS

Between 1919 and 1921, the US fur industry auctioned the pelts of a staggering 107,689,927 animals.

When Jacqueline Kennedy appeared in a leopard coat sold to her by Ben Kahn Furriers in New York in 1962, she launched a major trend. In 1968, the US imported 9,556 leopard skins, 1,283 cheetah skins, 13,516 jaguar skins and 133,064 ocelot skins. Similar numbers were imported into Europe.

QUINCE

A quince is a hard, acid fruit, shaped like an apple or pear, with a yellow skin. Quince preserves are still common in Greece and many other cultures and countries. Marmalade was originally a quince preserve, and the name derives from a type of quince, the Portuguese *marmelo*. The Greeks used the quince as an erotic metaphor. They had a verb – 'to quince' – which applied to things that swelled.

COSMIC APPOINTMENT

In 1965, Professor John McAleer from Massachusetts found a letter in his office from a convict, Billy Dickson, in response to a review the professor had written in the Boston *Globe*. McAleer wrote back and a correspondence developed which eventually produced a total of some 1,200 letters. Dickson was an eager student, but McAleer refrained from asking him what he had done or how much time he was doing.

After three months Dickson wrote: 'I appreciate your never asking what I'm here for, but I think I should tell you. On June 12th, 1956, I held up the Centerville Trust and got away with $10,000. I took a bank officer as hostage but let her go a little while later, unharmed. They caught up with me two months later.'

That night McAleer told his wife: 'I know what Billy did. He's the guy that held up your sister.' McAleer's sister-in-law had been badly shaken by the experience and now McAleer was writing letters to the man responsible.

McAleer wrote to Dickson again: 'A friend at MIT, a probability expert, told me that life was filled with million-to-one chances waiting their turn to happen, but to me it seemed providential that our paths had crossed in this way.'

Prison authorities were worried by this unconventional correspondence, but the relationship continued, with Dickson beginning work on a novel about his Korean War experiences, aided by McAleer. By 1967, he had a 1,000-page manuscript, which proved unsaleable; Dickson was released on parole, and the book was temporarily forgotten while Dickson adjusted to life outside.

Then in 1973 Dickson was stabbed to death in an argument and McAleer determined to work the book into a publishable form, and eventually *Unit Pride* was sold. McAleer says of the whole saga: 'Life sometimes serves up odd coincidences that writers are unwilling to credit. When I told my friend, the historian Henry Bragdon, about how Billy and I met, he said, "That's what my father used to call a cosmic appointment." '

GOLD

If all the gold ever mined were made into a solid cube, it would be 18 yards (16.4 metres) high and would weigh about 60,000 tonnes. New gold is being mined at the rate of about 1,600 tonnes a year.

The largest single stash of gold is the 13,000 tonnes of gold bricks stored in the vaults of the Federal Reserve Bank in New York. The vault is composed of 122 compartments protected by a 90-tonne steel cylinder door set in a 140-tonne frame. The largest stack, containing 107,000 gold bars, is known as 'the wall of gold' by workers in the bank.

In 1985, officials at the state mint factory in Perth, Australia, reported that, during 86 years of refining at the plant, some 1,000 ounces (28 kgs) of gold had vaporized and that the walls and ceiling would have to be smelted to separate the $A500,000 ($340,000)-worth of gold from the brickwork. The factory was relocated.

In 1986, a Swiss bank installed a gold-dispensing machine which delivered either 0.3-ounce (10-gm) gold bars or a choice of four gold coins in velvet-lined boxes for those requiring bullion outside normal banking hours.

In 1958, the Rhodia Company, a US subsidiary of the international chemical company Rhône-Poulenc, announced the development of a new scent film process. Since then, a number of 'smellies' have been produced. In 1965, a Chicago movie theatre showed an 11-minute Smellovision picture that featured a number of atmospheres and smells – including that of a wet dog – all controlled by an electronic 'memory drum'. In 1967, the San Sebastian Film Festival featured an entry called *Catalof*, a silent film accompanied by the smells of strawberry, violet and wintergreen.

In 1981 John Waters's *Polyester* (starring Divine and Tab Hunter) was released in Odorama. The audience was instructed to use a scratch-and-sniff card at key points in the film. Smells included pizza, a skunk, unpleasant bedroom smells, new leather and gas – the latter linked to scenes of two suicide attempts.

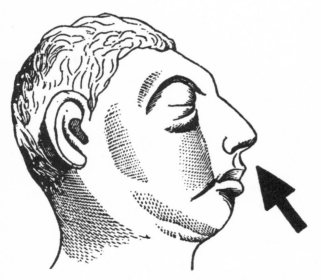

International Flavours & Fragrances is a highly successful but highly discreet New York-based firm that specializes in artificially 'creating' new and exotic tastes and aromas. They find the smells that companies want for their products using combinations of 6,000 ingredients.

IFF has produced a spruce-balsam smell for the Hall of North American Forests in the American Museum of Natural History, and the smell of 'salt air' for a marine museum in Florida. A restaurateur in California got them to produce the smells of baked ham and Dutch apple, which he sprays from aerosol cans to make his restaurant smell more enticing. They have even produced a special bottle – aptly labelled 'Cave' – that replicates the smells of moss, of dankness and of bats.

An olfactory 'blind spot' is called an anosmia, and almost everybody has one of the more than 100 known types. One of the most widely studied of these is the smell of androsterone, a steroid found in boar's saliva, human perspiration, bacon, celery and truffles. It is odourless to nearly half the population; those who can smell it describe it as being both musky and sweet, like urine or sweat.

How we smell things still eludes precise scientific definition. We know in principle that molecules in the air are picked up by receptors on the surface of cells inside the nose. These receptors trigger off signals that register in the part of the brain responsible for the sense of smell.

There are 25 million of these smell receptors located in a small patch at the top of each nostril passage. Fewer than a dozen molecules are sufficient to excite a receptor.

Odours are made up of bulk ingredients and trace ingredients. Only one part in a billion separates the taste of a grapefruit from that of an orange.

A whiff of peppermint makes you alert while a sniff of lily of the valley can relax you. Both smells will help you work better.

According to the *Bulletin of the Chemical Society of Japan*, a team of scientists has devised a method of weighing smells. On the basis that odorous molecules are readily absorbed by fats and oils, they coated an electronic microbalance with an oily film, sealed it inside an air-tight container and then injected a variety of smells. The nanograms of odour absorbed were thus weighed. They were able to show that the more the smell weighed, the more intensely it was experienced by human subjects.

Attar of roses, produced in a fold of the mountains in Bulgaria, is the oldest, rarest and most precious perfume invented or extracted by man. Forty million petals make just 2 lbs (1 kg) of oil.

Schizophrenia is commonly accompanied by a distinctive odour.

There are 15 great 'noses' in the perfume world, while a hundred others are highly rated. Ninety-five per cent of them are French; most are male, with ancestral roots in Grasse, a hill town inland from the Côte d'Azur. These 'noses' have the ability to memorize some 4,000 basic smells, both natural and synthetic, from which perfumes are constructed.

The best-selling scent of all time, Chanel No. 5, was created by the 'nose' of Ernest Beaux in the 1920s.

ZIPS

Better known for inventing the sewing machine, Elias Howe also took out the first patent for an automatic, continuous clothing closure but he never put it on the market.

The credit went instead to Whitcomb L. Judson, who in 1893 filed a patent entitled 'Clasp Locker or Unlocker for Shoes' and went on to found the Universal Fastener Company. Sales were poor because the fastener had a tendency to pop open at unexpected moments.

In 1904 they changed the company name to the Automatic Hook and Eye Company and began selling a new fastener called C-Curity.

The first item containing a zip to be mass-manufactured appeared in 1917. It was a money belt made by a New York tailor, which was popular with sailors during the First World War. By 1918 the fasteners were installed in 10,000 Navy flying suits.

The world's largest maker of zips is YKK, a $2 billion-a-year Japanese corporation, which is also the country's biggest manufacturer of aluminium building materials.

YKK – short for Yoshida Kogyo K.K. – controls 28–30 per cent of the global zipper market, and has 42 plants and 100 sales offices in 39 countries. Its office workers all wear light-grey windbreakers with eight zips. YKK has a plant in Swaziland.

The company has promoted the use of zips in fishing nets and oil-spill booms, and special zips for use in extreme cold, under water and with corrosive chemicals. It has even developed zippered plastic casts for bone fractures.

The Astroturf in the Houston Astrodome is held together with 8,000 zips.

Dr Danny Steinberg, a psychologist at the Japanese Surugadai University, applied in 1989 for a patent on a device called Zip Sure. Electrical contacts on a zip fastener set off an alarm if the trouser fly is left open for more than one minute. A second set of contacts on the waistband deactivates the system when the trousers are removed.

IVES'S INSURANCE

The American composer Charles Ives spent most of his working life as an insurance salesman. He authored such revolutionary pamphlets as *Life Insurance Scientifically Determined* and *The Amount to Carry and How to Carry It.*

KAZARIAN

Armenian Edward Kazarian is famed for his incredible miniatures. Carved with the aid of a microscope and a tool of his own design, which uses a speck of diamond dust as the cutting point, he has produced remarkable works. These include paintings of the Statue of Liberty, the Kremlin, the Bering Strait and the dove of peace on grains of rice, and a tiny sculpture of Charlie Chaplin's tramp framed in the eye of a needle.

After the Indian Government had given the Soviet Union a present of a needle with seven elephants carved on it, the Russians called on him to devise a suitable present in return. He polished a hair with diamond dust, hollowed it out, and inserted 300 carved elephants inside it.

Originally a violin-maker, Kazarian was asked to scale down an instrument for a four-year-old girl. It sounded so good that he then made a still smaller violin, 2 inches (50 mm) long. This led him to make an even smaller one, just half an inch (14 mm) long and weighing 0.017 ounces (0.5 gm). From then on he was hooked on the challenge of making tiny objects.

On one occasion he made an ivory opera house that sat on the point of a needle. Museum visitors reported seeing people moving about inside. These turned out to be microbes eating the ivory, so Kazarian redid it in plastic.

The world's leading expert on curses is Reinhold Aman, the founder of the International Research Center for Verbal Aggression, which publishes a scholarly journal, *Maledicta*.

Among the curses he has collected, which includes material in more than 200 languages dating back over 5,000 years, are a 3,000-year-old Egyptian hieroglyphic curse, a modern Ghanaian curse which describes a man's sexual organ as being 'as bent as the gearshaft of a Mercedes Benz', and the Esperanto curse 'fiulaco', which means 'disgusting person'.

Y

This is the name of a town in northern France situated near the banks of the River Somme. It is pronounced *ee-grec*. The natives call themselves Les Ypsiloniens or Les Yaciens. People in the surrounding areas call them Yroquois, Yennes or Yxiloniens.

No one is sure where the name came from. Mayor François Delacour researched it and came to the conclusion that it dates from 300 years ago when a sign was put up to indicate a fork in the road. He has found no other towns with just one letter as their names, but has located Oo and Wy in France, Au and Oy in Germany, Bo, Al and Ed in Norway, Ii in Finland and Ur in Iraq. Switzerland has an Au, Gy, Lu and Ob.

CHOCOLATE

Sandra Boynton, author of *Chocolate: The Consuming Passion,* justifies her title by claiming that a substance found in chocolate – phenylethylamine – is virtually identical to a chemical produced in the brains of infatuated lovers. It also contains theobromine, a stimulant that produces endomorphines in the brain.

Experiments at Yale University have shown that the smell of chocolate helps people to remember words more efficiently. The same was found to be true of mothballs.

In 1983, the great American Chocolate Festival was held at the Hotel Hershey, on the intersection of Cocoa and Chocolate Avenues in Hershey, Pennsylvania, home of the famous US chocolate

bars. (Milton Snavlely Hershey founded his factory with a $1 million fortune he had amassed, built a town around it, and with the profits founded a school for underprivileged children. The school now owns the company and a large part of the town.)

Chocolate News, a bi-monthly newsletter, has 16,000 subscribers, including Carl Sagan and Nancy Kissinger. It is printed on milk chocolate-coloured paper and smells like the topic it covers.

Two-ounce (57-gm) hunks of solid milk chocolate shaped like a human nose are sold by a company in Los Angeles called Brown-Nose Chocolate.

For thousands of years before the Spanish Conquest, Mexicans used unsweetened chocolate as a psychoactive drug to heighten religious experience and give a feeling of health and well-being. The scientific name for the chocolate plant, *Theobroma*, means 'godfood', a link to its sacred past.

Chocolate was a privilege restricted to adult males of royal birth. The Itza Indians made an exception to this rule – they fed it to their sacrificial victims, believing that it would magically turn their hearts to chocolate, providing a fit offering for the gods, once torn out of their living bodies.

Louis XVI of France had a Court Officer with the title 'Chocolatier to the King'.

The first chocolate-house in London was opened by a Frenchman in 1657 in Queen's Head Alley, Bishopsgate Street. It was called the Coffee Mill and Tobacco Roll, two products it didn't sell. Along with coffee-houses, chocolate-houses formed the basis of English clubs. The 'Cocoa Tree' Club, for instance, was a famous centre for the literati, including Edward Gibbon and Byron among its members.

In December 1986, sanitation workers in Bnei Brak near Tel Aviv extracted more than a ton of chocolate that had mysteriously jammed sewers. The clean-up cost £93,000 ($132,000).

Britons, the leading European consumers of chocolate, each spend £60 ($85) a year on it, a total of £3 billion ($4.2b). An estimated five million of them are chocaholics – people who eat more than the average *per capita* consumption of four bars a week.

One and a half ounces (42 gms) of chocolate contains nine per cent of the US daily recommended allowance of calcium and riboflavin, six per cent of the protein, three per cent of the iron, 2.4 per cent of the vitamin A and 200 calories. Chocolate does not cause acne but it does give you an instant energy boost because it contains glucose.

Skull Crushers – 2-inch (50-mm)-long chocolate skulls that ooze red fondant when bitten – were invented by the small family firm of Alma Confectionery in Kirkcaldy, Fife. In the first year (1983) they sold 50 million in Britain, sent 750,000 to South Africa (along with three million strawberry-flavoured pink elephants) and clinched a $300,000 deal to launch them in the USA.

The Canadian Cold Buster is a chocolate bar designed to combat hypothermia; it is formulated so that it helps the body to use fat more efficiently in the cold. The bar took 15 years and $750,000 funding by the Canadian Department of Defence to develop. Its efficacy was tested by students at the University of Alberta, who spent six hours in temperatures of -50°F (-10°C) wearing only T-shirts and shorts; those who ate the bar were shown to have a 50 per cent greater tolerance of the cold.

TWINS

Seven thousand pairs of twins, one in every 83 births, are born in Britain each year. The rate is rising as more women are having babies later in life, which increases the chances of having twins.

Millville in Ohio changed its name to Twinsburg in 1819 when the twins Moses and Aaron Wilcox, general traders from Connecticut, bought 4,000 acres (1,620 hectares) of land in the area and gave 20 of them to the town, providing its name was changed. They both died on the same day and are buried side by side in the town's Locust Grove cemetery. The town came to prominence in 1976 when the first festival for twins was staged there; in 1990 some 5,000 sets of twins attended, including nine pairs from Russia. Plans are now being laid for a twin research library, a twin museum and a hall of fame.

The first successful operation to separate Siamese twins – Folke and Tstitske de Vries – took place in Holland on 3 June 1955.

The first known case of multiple personality in identical twins was identified by Drs Arlene Levine and Robert S. Mayer at New York's Odyssey House drug facility. Each had six personalities that were twins of the other six personalities. The doctors believe this was triggered in the younger twin by an incestuous relationship with her father, himself diagnosed as a multiple personality. The second twin developed her own multiple personality in order to relate fully to her twin.

Identical twins Pat and Pauline married John and Peter Collister, who are also identical twins, in a double ceremony in 1984, and subsequently gave birth to their first babies in the same hospital within minutes of each other.

Linda Whicher gave birth to her third successive set of twins in July 1983; the odds against this are 50 million to one.

Richard Dunning, a British advertising art director, paid an unknown sum ('it wasn't cheap') to buy a hole 90 feet (27 metres) deep and 300 feet (91 metres) wide from a French farmer, Georges Delphanque, in 1977. Mr Dunning claims his hole is historic, having been created by British sappers using 60 tonnes of dynamite on 1 July 1916 – the first day of the Battle of the Somme.

In New York in 1978, 37,000 potholes were reported in the city's roads, of which the city managed to repair only one-fifth; 4,700 claimants for pothole injuries were paid an average of $3,000 each in compensation.

In 1980 a new city ordnance was passed preventing anyone from suing the city over a pothole, unless the authorities had been informed and had 15 days to patch it up. Five hundred lawyers responded by forming the Pothole and Sidewalk Protection Corporation, which began a search of the city's 13,000 miles (21,000 kms) of streets and sidewalks and began mapping something in the order of a million potholes. For a fee they then informed potential litigants whether their pothole provided grounds to sue.

In 1985 the city paid out more than £4 million ($5.6m) for pothole-related injuries and in 1986 there were a reported 94,147 potholes in the city.

Every 15 seconds someone somewhere in Britain starts digging a hole in a road. Every day 5,000 new holes are started, and 1,250 times a day pipes and cables are damaged by people digging these holes. Computer modelling of what lies beneath our streets and coordination of hole-digging may alleviate the problem in future.

DEEPER AND DEEPER

The deepest hole in the world is a well near Murmansk in the Kola Peninsula of the former Soviet Union, 155 miles (250 kms) north of the Arctic Circle. Drilling began in May 1970, it reached 7 1/2 miles (12 kms) on 28 December 1983, and drilling still continues. The first formal results, presented at the 27th International Geological Union in Moscow in August 1984, revealed that large amounts of water had been discovered at great depths in the Earth's crust. The rocks at such depths are 2,700 million years old.

Every time the drill bit wears out, the entire drill string has to be recovered in order to change it. To date over 15,500 miles (25,000 kms) of pipe have passed through the well mouth.

Even this hole is a mere pinprick, extending only one-third of the way into the Earth's crust.

The second deepest hole in the world is the Bertha Rogers well in Oklahoma, which is 6 miles (9.67 kms) deep. For the record: the world's deepest open-cast mine is half a mile (746 metres) deep; the deepest water well, in Montana, is 1 1/3 miles (2.2 kms); the deepest steam well, in California, is 1 3/4 miles (2.7 kms); the deepest mine, the Western Deep in South Africa, is 2 1/2 miles (3.8 kms).

The German Continental Drilling Project is boring a 6-mile (10-km) hole into the Earth's crust near the Bavarian town of Windischeschenbach, close to the Czech border.

This government-backed project should be complete by 1994 and is expected to cost more than DM 500 million ($300m). It is being bored using the biggest drilling rig in the world, which is 270 feet (83 metres) high. The emphasis of the whole project is one of pure research, to gain an understanding of the Central European Crust, but there should be technical spin-offs in the form of improved drilling techniques, which may make the exploitation of geothermal power look more promising.

On 12 May 1992, no fewer than 30 climbers from five expeditions reached the summit of Everest.

Climber Wolfgang Gorter was so angry that Germany's highest mountain, Zugspitze, was only 9,724 feet (2,964 metres) high that he built a concrete tower on top to make it a 3,000-metre mountain.

Aconcagua, in Argentina, at 22,633 feet (6,900 metres) the tallest mountain in the Western Hemisphere and the forty-third highest mountain in the world, has the reputation of being a killer, surrounded as it is by vicious, changeable weather. Twelve of the 64 known and identified victims of the mountain lie buried in a special 'cemetery of the defeated' at its foot. Its strange microclimate causes hallucinations; one experienced climber claimed he saw horses dancing on the summit, while another claimed there were paved roads and trees at the top.

Walter Poucher, who died at the age of 96 in August 1988, was chief perfumer at Yardleys for 30 years and a pre-eminent mountain photographer. His obituarist recalls: 'Poucher used to combine his two interests by wearing make-up and perfume in the mountains, a habit which disconcerted some of his self-consciously masculine climbing friends.'

'Munroists' are an élite band of climbers who have scaled each one of the 277 peaks of 3,000 feet (915 metres) or more in Scotland known as Munros. The Victorian mountaineer and landowner Sir Hugh Munro was the first to discover them all – until the 1880s it was believed there were only 30 of them – and he set out to climb them. He died in 1918 at the age of 62 with just two peaks unclimbed. The first man to complete them all was the Rev. Archibald Robertson. By 1991 the number of Munroists had exceeded 800. The longest recorded time to complete the climb is 57 years; the shortest three-and-a-half months, being claimed by Hamish Brown, who has done the Munro circuit six times. Munroists often find life flat and empty after achieving their goal; some go on to conquer the 233 'Corbetts' (2,500– 3,000 feet/760–915 metres) and the 86 'Donalds' (2,000–2,500 feet/610–760 metres).

In August 1986, Pascal Monel, a French pilot, became the first person to fly a micro-light aircraft to the 15,771-foot (4,800-metre) peak of Mont Blanc, Europe's highest mountain, during a week of celebrations for the 200th anniversary of the first ascent.

The fastest person to climb the mountain took eight hours and 28 minutes, and the youngest climber was an eight-year-old, who reached the summit in 1980. A motorcycle reached the top in 1922, and others have parachuted in, landed by helicopter and eaten a gourmet meal on the summit.

It is known locally as Chomolungma (Goddess Mother of the World), Chomolangma (Goddess of the Mountain Snows) or Sagarmatha (Goddess of the Wind). The British originally called it Peak XV after its position and height had been plotted, but in 1865 it was officially named Mount Everest after Sir George Everest, the Surveyor-General for India and chief architect of the Great Trigonometrical Survey of India.

Henry Haversham Godwin-Austen was not so fortunate: despite being the discoverer of K2 in 1886, his name refused to stick.

In 1987 an astronomy professor from Seattle named George Wallerstein declared that K2 was 32 feet (10 metres) higher than Everest; he had re-measured it using a satellite receiver which he had planted on the mountain the previous year. His announcement triggered off a furious burst of space-age measurement, with advocates competing from both camps. Italian climbers did an on-the-spot placement of receivers and the results have now been officially accepted: K2 is 13 feet (4 metres) smaller than previously thought at 28,239 feet 6 inches (8,607 metres) and Everest is 50 feet (15 metres) higher at 29,079 feet 6 inches (8,863 metres).

In 1988 a 101-year-old former lumberjack climbed Mount Fuji in three days, breaking his own record as the oldest person to scale Japan's tallest peak.

STAMPS

A black face appeared for the first time on a South African postage stamp in July 1983.

In Monaco you can use any stamp ever issued in the principality, and in France stamps are also valid indefinitely. In the US any stamp issued after 1849 can still be used. In England only new pence stamps can be used, though the law allows for the use of stamps back to one previous monarch.

Stanley Gibbons Ltd, the world's largest stamp dealers, estimate that there are between 40 and 100 million collectors worldwide. Chairman A.L. Michael claims that his biggest deal was for a collection of some 4,500,000 stamps, neatly arranged in 3,000 volumes. And his most outrageous – the purchase of 260 whisky cartons full of stamps from a man in New York who hoarded 26 tonnes of paper and thousands of broomstick handles in his basement during the First World War.

Collectors specialize. There is a man who has a complete set of the 30 to 40 stamps featuring pictures of seaweed, who remains optimistic about future issues. Another collects stamps with upside-down centres, another with penguins on. Dentists collect teeth stamps, inmates prison stamps and oculists eyeglass stamps.

Circus clown and pantomime artist Albert Schafer spent his life decorating objects with stamps. The results of his obsession can be seen in the Stamp Room, now housed in a museum in Great Yarmouth. Everything in the room – Toby jugs, paintings, plates, spinning wheels, chairs, tables, a piano – is carefully covered, often with very valuable stamps, like the Twopenny Blues used to form the hair ribbons in a portrait of Lady Hamilton. Schafer wrote more than 200 songs, and was a member of the world-famous Schafer Troupe, before an accident on the high wire forced his retirement and he was able to devote himself full-time to his obsession.

The most infamous philatelic forger of all time was an Italian, Jean de Sperati, who had an amazing knowledge of photography, printing, the chemistry of colours and the composition of paper and, in his lifetime, produced between 50,000 and 70,000 of what he termed his 'artistic reproductions'.

In 1953, when the British Philatelic Association heard that Sperati wanted to pass his knowledge on, it made a deal to buy him out, destroying his machinery and acquiring his reference collection, master blocks, and a typescript describing his methods, which the BPA has kept a closely guarded secret ever since. Sperati died in 1957.

For years, a pair of dice rested on a velvet cushion in the Desert Inn Casino, Las Vegas. The dice were used by a roller who made an incredible 28 passes at the craps table in June 1950, beating odds of ten million to one. Unfortunately, he only bet $2 on each throw and ended with $750 instead of the almost $300 million he would have won if he had let his winnings ride. The dice were lost during rebuilding.

A Spanish royal decree published in 1977 barred civil servants and military men who handle state funds, minors, drunks, madmen and convicts on parole from gambling in casinos.

El Gordo, 'the Fat One', is reputed to be the world's richest lottery. In 1973, the total prize money amounted to 1.19 billion pesetas ($10m). In 1989 it was 20,000 billion pesetas ($170m). Set up in 1763 by King Carlos III as an additional source of revenue for the Spanish state, it has been held every Christmas ever since.

In his book *The Newtonian Casino*, Thomas Bass relates how he was one of a group of computer science students at the University of California who set out to design a computer that could be worn secretly and used in a casino. The book claims they succeeded, producing a device that fitted inside a shoe and gave a 33 per cent return at the tables.

The system used three of these devices and two people, one as a predictor, one as a player. The predictor entered the data in the computer in his right shoe, using his big toe, and microtransmitters sent the data to the computer in the left shoe, which produced a prediction. This, in turn, was fed to the right shoe computer of the player – who placed the chips.

Doyne Farmer, who led the team, is now group leader in the Theoretical Division at the Los Alamos Laboratory in New Mexico.

Alex Bird, who died in December 1991, was Britain's most successful racing punter, who made his fortune betting on the outcome of photo finishes. It used to be possible to lay a bet in the five minutes between a neck-and-neck finish and the announcement of the results. Bird always stood right on the line: 'I never took my eyes off it. I couldn't even blink. I didn't see the horses, only their noses. But my real secret was that, in a photo finish, you get an optical illusion that the far horse is fractionally in front. So I always backed the horse nearest me.' In this way he achieved an unbroken run of 500–600 winners and made more than £1 million ($1.42m). The system has now been changed, denying anyone the chance of emulating this feat.

Under US law, American Indian reservations have the unique status of mini-governments, which includes exemption from many state and federal gaming laws. As a result, bingo halls and casinos are springing up on many reservations and a National Indian Gaming Association has been established. In 1990 their combined income was estimated at $1 billion. One of the most profitable is the Little Six Casino, at Prior Lake in Minnesota, which generates an income of $175,000 per head per year for each of the 90 registered members of the Shakopee Sioux tribe.

Bingo is Britain's second most popular pastime after fishing. Some 2.8 million people, mostly women over 45 years old, play regularly; on a Saturday night, one million gamblers turn up at the 1,000 or so bingo clubs around the country. They spend £618 million ($877m) a year in stake money, an average of £7.70 ($11) per night per player.

One of the most extraordinary architectural phenomena in the USA between the world wars was the construction of hundreds of 'atmospheric cinemas', giant picture palaces which included the Siamese Byzantine in Detroit, the Andalusian Baroque in Tampa and, most spectacular of all, the Fox in Atlanta.

This latter was originally conceived and constructed in the 1920s as a Masonic Hall for the Shriners, but spiralling costs forced them to go into partnership with William K. Fox, reserving the right to use the 5,000-seater at least six times a year.

Designed by a firm whose main stock-in-trade was churches and telephone exchanges, it was built to embody the entire scope of Islamic art, and came complete with turrets, a minaret, dressing-rooms inspired by the discoveries of Tutankhamun's tomb in 1922, and a screen flanked by an emulation of a fortified Muslim town with gatehouses and battlements.

These 'atmospheric' cinemas, first created by John Eberson, were designed to give the illusion of an outdoor courtyard under a moonlit sky. A notice found in the projection room of a cinema in Minnesota read: 'Please do not turn on the clouds until the show starts. Be sure the stars are turned off when leaving.'

KAR-MI

Kar-Mi, whose real name was Joseph B. Hallworth, toured the US with a 15-minute act in the early 1900s. Among his tricks was one where he 'Swallows a Loaded Gun Barrel . . . and Shoots a Cracker from a Man's Head'. It is said that he eventually died of stomach cancer as a result.

APHRODISIACS

An exhaustive search by anthropologist George Armelagos of the University of Florida, co-author of *Consuming Passions*, has failed to discover a genuine aphrodisiac. Having examined the use of thousands of substances including hippopotamus snout, shark's fins, prunes in Elizabethan times, tree bark in West Africa and the overrated potency of champagne, he concludes that the brain is 'the most important sexual organ'.

TICKER-TAPE

Ticker-tape parades, a distinctive New York way of honouring national heroes, began in 1927 to celebrate the achievements of the aviator Charles Lindbergh. Since then there have been 35 parades, the success being judged by the weight of waste paper collected afterwards. The biggest was in 1945 to celebrate victory over Japan (5,438 tonnes), followed by that for astronaut John Glenn in 1961 (3,474 tonnes), and the New York Jets winning the World Series in 1969 (1,225 tonnes).

When the Pope visited New York ten years later, only 43 tonnes of rubbish resulted. This was partly because the old 'ticker' machines have been replaced by computer terminals, and partly because many office buildings are completely air-conditioned and their windows won't open.

Soon the parades may be a thing of the past. When 20 of the 52 US hostages rescued from Iran paraded through New York on 30 January 1981, more than 100 miles (161 kms) of tape had to be specially ordered from a firm in Connecticut.

Born Harry Relph, he was the sixteenth child of a publican who ran the Blacksmith's Arms in Cudham, Kent. Born with two extra fingers, he stopped growing at the age of ten. Despite these physical disadvantages he became one of the greatest comedians of the music hall, admired by such diverse people as Nijinsky, Max Wall, Jacques Tati, Stravinsky (who wrote a quartet in his honour), J.B. Priestley and Sir Ralph Richardson.

His new name originated because he was fat as a child, and was known as Little Tichbourne. This was derived from a famous court case of the 1870s when an immensely fat (400-lb/185-kg) butcher from Wagga Wagga in Australia claimed he was the rightful heir to the wealthy Tichbourne estates in Hampshire. He was sent to prison and, on his release, toured the music halls. The word titch has since passed into the language.

Married three times, a comic genius who was one of Chaplin's early influences, Little Tich was dapper and graceful, elfin and bizarre. He was famed for his Big Boot dance, which he performed in footwear that looked like a cross between flippers and winkle-pickers and that were half his own height in length.

According to the painter Walter Sickert, Little Tich used to go on outings to Paris and Dieppe with Toulouse-Lautrec, who was almost the same age and the same height (4 feet 6 inches/1.4 metres), frightening women with their 'objectionable behaviour'. Lautrec's portrait of Tich has disappeared.

BLACKBIRD

Nicknamed for its matt-black, heat-resistant exterior, the Lockheed SR-71 *Blackbird* was the original 'stealth' aircraft, its curved surfaces and narrow fuselage being designed to reflect very little radar.

An unarmed strategic photographic and electronic reconnaissance aircraft, it was intended to succeed the U-2 as the premier US spyplane (it proved to be complementary) and was specifically designed to monitor breaches of the Nuclear Non-Proliferation Treaty and 'hot spots' around the world.

It flew faster and higher than any other plane in the world, at altitudes of more than 80,000 feet (24,500 metres) and speeds of more than 2,700 mph (4,345 km/h). One Blackbird flew from New York to London in one hour, 54 minutes and 56.4 seconds. Its two engines produce a thrust equivalent to the *Queen Mary*. At supersonic speeds, its titanium skin – as thin as that of a soft drinks can – expanded and changed colour to deep blue as the temperature rose to 500°F (260°C), while the nose cone glowed red.

Each plane flew for only around 200 hours a year, mostly in order to keep the crew proficient. Packed with sensory equipment, it could scan 60,000 square miles (155,500 sq metres) of earth per hour. It could photograph a car number-plate from 15 miles (24 kms) up, and outfly virtually any missile; none of the 30 or so Blackbirds (the exact number remained a secret) was ever shot down in more than 1,000 missions.

The fleet, which formed a single squadron of 30 or more planes, was mothballed in 1990 due to defence cutbacks and the advent of sophisticated satellites. In one of its final flights, a Blackbird flew from Los Angeles to Washington, DC in 68 minutes and 17 seconds, smashing the previous record of four hours, twelve minutes. Its average speed was 2,112.52 mph (3,400 km/h).

The Scottish and Newcastle Breweries have been sponsoring archaeological excavations in Egypt, to help discover the recipe for a 3,400-year-old beer drunk during the reign of King Tutankhamun.

Clues have come from an ancient brewery unearthed near the ancient Egyptian capital of Tell el Armana, where giant brewing jars that held $10^1/_2$ – 13 gallons (40–50 litres) of beer have been found, and from paintings in tombs that provide a visual record of the brewing process.

Further evidence was provided by three grains of wheat found in the King's tomb itself. These grains were examined under an electron microscope and provided vital clues as to how the wheat was malted.

The evidence suggests that the Pharoah's beer was made by soaking the grain, from a wild wheat called emmer *(Triticum dicoccum)*, until it germinated. This was ground and strained to form a mash to which yeast was added. This 'sourdough' was lightly baked, crumbled and mixed with water, and then left inside large jars to brew. The beer was then probably flavoured with herbs, cinammon or fruit.

S&N were due to produce 2,000 bottles of the newly-brewed ancient tipple for sale to collectors in 1993.

Porter – a strong, mellow and fruity beer – was first brewed in Britain in the middle of the eighteenth century and became the country's most popular ale, until after the First World War, when it was replaced by bitter.

In 1991 a chemist at Brewlab, which specializes in analysis for the brewing industry, succeeded in culturing yeast taken from a cargo of 500 bottles of porter on board a sunken sailing barge that had gone down in 1825 off the south coast of England. With this and an 1850 recipe, he produced his first batch of

Flag Porter, the forerunner of such stout ales as Guinness, Murphy's and Beamish.

Brewlab is hoping to plunder other 'bottle wrecks', including one containing a cargo of champagne known to be on the seabed off the Scottish coast.

Brewlab has also worked to develop an ancient Viking beer, launched in Sunderland in 1992, named Civic Pride.

The beer owes its re-emergence to the discovery of some yeast by Michael Jackson, presenter of the BBC series *Beerhunter,* in a remote farmhouse in Norway. This yeast had been passed down from generation to generation since Viking times.

The yeast produced a hot, spicy, unpleasant-tasting brew, which had to be tweaked to suit modern taste. The result is, by all accounts, a delicious and potent ale.

BULAWAYO BROTHEL-BLASTER

A dissatisfied customer at a brothel in Bulawayo, Zimbabwe, blew it up with TNT in February 1990, killing a 15-year-old girl and demolishing half of the establishment's 64 rooms. Its 200 prostitutes had a notorious reputation for seriously ill-treating clients.

LITERARY COINCIDENCES

Crime reporter Ann Rule signed a contract with an American publishing company to write a book about a maniacal mass-murderer who, police claimed, may have killed more than 30 young women in three states in a violent, bloody manner. The man who was eventually convicted of the murders turned out to be a friend of Rule's, Ted Bundy.

Journalist Peter Watson, fresh from writing a book about coincidences in the lives of identical twins, posed as an art dealer called John Blake in order to try to recover a stolen Caravaggio, and wrote about his experiences in *The Caravaggio Conspiracy*, which was published on 6 January 1984. Two days earlier a book entitled *The Caravaggio Obsession* by Oliver Banks was also published. It concerned the fictional adventures of an art dealer trying to locate a stolen Caravaggio. The dealer's name in the story was Richard Blake.

Following a *Sunday Times* story on coincidences by Arthur Koestler in 1973, readers were invited to submit their own experiences. The £100 ($140) first prize was won by 12-year-old Nigel Parker with the following. In the summer of 1884, his great-grandfather's cousin was a cabin-boy on a yawl named the *Mignonette,* when she foundered. There were only four survivors left in an open boat, and the three senior crew members eventually ate the cabin boy, whose name was Richard Parker. The case was reported in *The Times* (28 October 1884). In 1838, Edgar Allan Poe had written a story called 'The Narrative of Arthur Gordon Pym of Nantucket'. It told of a parallel set of circumstances in which an unfortunate seaman was also eaten. His name was Richard Parker.

In an article entitled 'Mere Coincidence?' Robert Anton Wilson cited the following example: 'When Norman Mailer began his novel *Barbary Shore* there was no Russian spy in it. As he worked on it, a Russian spy became a minor character. As the work progressed, the spy became the dominant character. After the novel was finished, the Immigration Service arrested a man who lived one flight below Mailer in the same building. He was Colonel Rudolf Abel, named as the top Russian spy in the United States at that time.'

WATER

The most pervasive – and most essential – compound on Earth, water is the third most abundant substance in the universe (after hydrogen and helium). Our bodies are 65 per cent water; that of the frog is 78 per cent and the jellyfish 95 per cent.

Water has unusual electrical properties. Each molecule consists of one oxygen and two hydrogen atoms, so arranged as to give a slightly positive charge on one side and a slightly negative charge on the other. Since each attracts its opposite, any water molecule will readily 'join hands' with any nearby molecule, regardless of its charge. It is for this reason that so many substances dissolve in water.

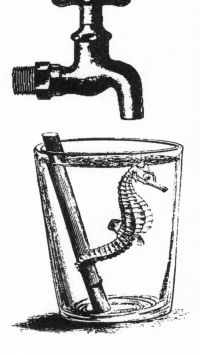

Most matter contracts as its temperature drops, since molecular motion is reduced. Water, however, follows this rule only until it begins to solidify into ice. At this point, the molecules rearrange themselves into a porous, more space-consuming configuration – causing the overall volume to increase. Sealed iron flasks a quarter of an inch (6 mm) thick have been known to explode violently when the water inside them was rapidly frozen.

When ice thaws, its molecular structure collapses again and the volume decreases. A pound of cold water is therefore smaller and denser than a pound of hot water. A pound of ice is larger and less dense than either.

In 1984, Soviet scientists found a drop of water trapped inside a small prism of rock crystal in the Pamir Mountains in Central Asia. It is estimated to be 50 million years old.

EMPIRE STATE BUILDING

Few people realize that in order to build the Empire State, what was then the largest hotel in the world had to be knocked down. The story goes like this.

William Waldorf Astor built the Waldorf Hotel on the site formerly occupied by his own huge house. Opened in March 1893, it was 13 storeys tall, with 530 rooms and 350 private baths. Soon afterwards John Jacob Astor IV, who lived next door, pulled down his house and set out to outdo his cousin by building the Astoria Hotel with 17 storeys. The two were eventually connected to form the largest hotel in the world: with 1,000 rooms and 765 private baths, it opened in November 1897.

The idea for the Empire State Building came from the magnate John Jacob Raskob, who acquired the site in secret and demolished the hotel in October 1929, with little public fanfare.

According to Robert Jungk, 'Never before had so gigantic a building been erected in so short a time in the traffic centre of a city . . . Every strut, every stone was to be brought and fitted at an appointed date. Every lorry with building materials had to time its hours of arrival. If it came only a little too late it might have to wait a week for the next chance to unload.'

The huge project had its own finance minister and separate departments for underground work, electrical installations, purchase of raw materials and erection of steel scaffolding. The only thing that was not planned for was the 1929 Wall Street Crash.

The building's construction used 10 million bricks and 60,000 tonnes of steel and there are 102 floors, 6,500 windows, 1,860 steps, 61 passenger- and six freight-lifts. The building has its own fire brigade and post office and the biggest postcard and souvenir shop in the world. It was inaugurated on 1 May 1931, but for many years two-thirds of the offices remained vacant and it became known as 'the largest ghost city in the world'. From 1941 onwards, however, the investment began to pay off.

'Anti-suicide police' were first installed in 1946, after 17 people had leapt to their deaths. These included the diamond merchant Solomon Rosbach who jumped on 9 May 1946, leaving this message: 'No above, no below. So I jump.'

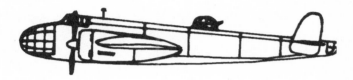

On a foggy day in July 1945, a twin-engined B-52 bomber crashed into the 79th floor, killing the three-man crew, burning or crushing to death ten workers employed by the Catholic War Relief Services, and injuring 26 others.

A dictaphone roll recorded the scene. Jungk reports: 'A man's voice could be heard dictating a business letter, his scream of fright quickly drowned by the noise of motors, shrill telephone rings, cries for help. It was a sound picture of the end of the world . . .'

The cables of one elevator were severed and the lift plunged 1,000 feet (300 metres), burying itself 3 feet (1 metre) into the ground. The woman operator survived.

Aviation fuel showered down on the surrounding streets and flames reached as high as the observatory of the building, 1,050 feet (320 metres) above Fifth Avenue, when the plane's gasoline tanks exploded.

The victims' relatives gained only modest compensation after an eight-year wait. The sole remnant of the tragedy is a small blackened crevice below the 79th-floor windows, which is visible only to the window cleaners – who, like most members of the trade in New York – are almost all of Ukrainian origin.

The Rock Harmonicon was a two-tier xylophone contraption composed of banks of selected rocks, all carefully tuned. Built by stonemason Joseph Richardson over a period of 13 years, it made its début in the 1840s at the Egyptian Hall on the south side of Piccadilly. Under the billing of 'Messrs Richardson and Sons, Original Monster Rock Band', the maker and his three boys played it using mallets with tips the size and shape of cricket balls. It had a range of five and a half octaves, with sounds from the warble of a lark to the 'deep bass of a funeral bell'. Richardson defined his instrument as 'the resource of a shipwrecked Mozart'. A duplicate instrument, known as the Lithophone and made of stone from the Skiddau Mountain in the Lake District, was used by Daniel Till and Children on several tours of the US in the late nineteenth century. He went bankrupt in 1881 and it was purchased by a museum in New Jersey.

The Therminovox was the first electronic instrument. It was developed by Russian acoustical engineer Lev Thermin, who demonstrated it personally to Lenin in the early 1920s. It consisted of an electrically tuned circuit with a loudspeaker; you changed the pitch of the tone by moving your hand towards and away from an aerial sticking out of the top.

Thermin toured Europe and America with his instrument and became the darling of high society. You can hear the Therminovox on some soundtracks recorded by Bernard Herrman, who often worked with Alfred Hitchcock.

Californian musician Chris Roberts bought the bullet-scarred bass used by Jack Lemmon in *Some Like It Hot* in a Los Angeles music shop and took it with him to the villages of Western Papua New

Guinea. He played the Min villagers who lived there Bach on the instrument they called his *tiringmingi* (hollow slapping) and, in return, they sang him more than a hundred of their songs, which had never been recorded before.

Inax, a leading Japanese manufacturer of lavatory bowls and wash basins, made a ceramic violin, which was used in its first public performance at a concert by the Nagoya City Orchestra in May 1989. The tone of the instrument is reported to be good, and it does not warp, but it is a bit heavier than the traditional wooden instrument.

Bösendorfer make the world's largest and most expensive piano. It is 8¹/₂ feet (2.6 metres) long, has nine extra notes in the bass, and costs £35,000 ($50,000).

The piano was invented by Italian harpsichordmaker Bartolomeo Cristofori in Florence in about 1709.

A few of the instruments featured in a US newsletter called *Experimental Musical Instruments* are: the Ostrich-Egg Ocarina, the Pikasso Guitar (which looks like several guitars wrestling), the Seaweed Horn, and the Dachsophon (a strip of wood, clamped to the table and sawed with a bow, which makes noises like a nursing piglet).

The 7-foot (2.1-metre)-long serpent is, as the name suggests, a curvaceous woodwind instrument made of walnut wood, covered in fine leather, tipped with brass, and with an ebony mouthpiece. The sound it makes has been described as 'gruff as a snorting buffalo, as sinister as wind among tombstones'.

The man responsible for its modern revival is Andrew van der Beek, founder of the London Serpent Trio, which gives concerts around the world.

He also occasionally plays the world's only known contra-bass C serpent, called the Anaconda, which was carved by Joseph and Richard Wood, two Yorkshire hand-loom weavers, around 1840. It is 15 feet 7 inches (4.7 metres) long and has a diameter at the bell end of $7^1/_2$ inches (19 cms).

In 1988 a team of chemists at Cambridge University claimed to have discovered the secret ingredient that gives the musical instruments made by Antonio Stradivari their exceptional tone – a layer of volcanic ash called pozzolana, found in the Cremona district of Italy where Stradivari lived. This ash was an excellent primer for the varnish and added strength to the instruments, many of which are still being played 300 years after he made them.

The kazoo originated in Africa, where it was used not as a musical instrument but as a weapon of intimidation, disguising the voice so as to imitate the voices of the dead. According to Barbara Stewart, author of *How to Kazoo*, 'The penalty for disclosure of this secret was death, which made it hard for the anthropologists to get the truth.'

Charlie 'Boom Boom' Marsh is in demand throughout the US as the cannon player who supplies the blasts and explosions in Beethoven's *Wellington's Victory* and also Tchaikovsky's *1812 Overture*. He has three Civil War cannons, one three-quarter-size replica and 13 mortars. The Beethoven piece calls for 108 booms, the *1812* for 16 cannon blasts.

In November 1980, the Soviet record company Melodiya released a record of music produced on instruments fashioned from mammoth bones 20,000 years ago.

The first ski club in the world was founded in Australia in 1861.

What exactly are the Ashes? Legend has it they are the remains of a burnt bail presented to Ivo Bligh, the England captain, in 1883. In recent years other explanations have surfaced: that they are the remains of an Aborigine named King Cole, who died while touring England in 1868, or that they are the remains of a ball, not a bail. According to Bligh's former butler, a housemaid knocked the urn over, scattering the ashes, so he refilled it from the fireplace.

Stephane Peyron became the first person to windsurf solo across the Atlantic. It took him 47 days to cover the 3,300 nautical miles from New York to La Rochelle in France.

The 'father' of croquet was Walter James Whitmore who, from 1860 onwards, devoted himself to promoting the game and devising a set of laws and a code of tactics. He also invented such devices as a safety-valve for kettles, a shoe-horn for galoshes and a bootlace winder.

Canadian Hilda Strike lost the 100 metres sprint at the 1932 Olympics by centimetres to a Polish-born American, Stella Walsh. When Walsh died in 1980, caught in the crossfire during an armed robbery in Cleveland, the autopsy revealed she was a man.

Preliminary studies in the Amazon suggest that ants represent about one-third of the entire animal biomass — the combined weight of all mammals, birds, fish and invertebrates, including insects. There may be, at any one time, one quadrillion (10^{15}) ants living on Earth — 200,000 ants for every human being. Together with termites, ants account for most of the turning of the Earth's topsoil, far more than either earthworms or human agriculture.

Some 8,800 ant species have been scientifically described, and it is thought that two to three times that number remain to be discovered.

On a single tree in the Peruvian rain forest, Edward O. Wilson (co-author with Bert Hölldobler of *The Ants*, the definitive ant opus) found 43 ant species belonging to 26 genera — almost equal to the entire ant fauna of Britain.

Ants are also a major factor in seed dispersal on every continent except Antarctica. More than 3,000 species, belonging to more than 60 families of flowering plants, are known to be distributed in this way and many more are sure to be discovered. These plants produce an elaiosome, a fat body that is near or attached to a seed; this lures the ants, which then carry the seed and the elaiosome back to their nests. The ant colony eats the elaiosome and discards the seed unharmed.

ONE IN A MILLION

Mrs Marva Drew, a 51-year-old housewife from Waterloo, Iowa, typed out every number from one to one million after her son's teacher told him it was impossible to count up to a million. It took her five years and 2,473 sheets of typing paper.

ST HELENA

St Helena is a 47-square-mile (122-sq-km) subtropical volcanic outcrop, 1,000 miles (1,610 kms) from the nearest landfall and 5,000 miles (8,500 kms) from Britain.

Most famous as the place where Napoleon I died in exile, it later served as a camp for prisoners from the Boer War.

The Governor of this, Britain's most isolated colony, lives in a Georgian mansion with four ancient tortoises in the garden named Emma, Myrtle, Freda and Jonathan. The latter is believed to be over 250 years old.

The local brew is Atlantic Ale. The mainstay of the economy was hemp string for the British Post Office until it was replaced by nylon string or rubber bands. Overnight the St Helenan economy collapsed. Now rampant flax covers two-thirds of the island.

The island's telephone directory is ten pages long.

St Helena has a sheriff, a registrar, a bishop and troops of boy scouts and girl guides. The only flat field on the island is used for cricket matches; the only town on the island, Jamestown, has 45 policemen.

The Russian postal authorities will not accept letters containing chewing-gum. Nigeria, Zimbabwe and Malawi ban aphrodisiacs by post, and many African countries ban Japanese shaving brushes. Afghanistan bans ashtrays. Guyana will not accept artificial Christmas trees.

The Swiss PTT (Post, Telephone and Telegraph) has a higher number of postal employees per head of population (1,641 inhabitants per postal employee) than anywhere else in the world. They also have 3,903 post offices for a population of 6.5 million. The legendary efficiency of the service is summed up by the following story.

On 3 November 1950, an Air India Superconstellation flying from Calcutta to Geneva hit Mont Blanc and exploded, the contents of the plane being scattered over the landscape. Then in June 1978, a group of French *gendarmerie* recruits on a training expedition 4,000 feet (1,220 metres) up on Mont Blanc's Bossons glacier found one of the plane's mail sacks containing 60 letters, which were perfectly preserved.

The sack went to Paris where the French authorities sorted the contents and contacted the Swiss PTT, who immediately despatched someone to pick up the 23 letters for Switzerland. Then began attempts to deliver them. Several commercial enterprises were still going and at the same address, but only one of the private addressees was still alive, Dr Martha Voegeli of Thun. The letter was from one of her colleagues at a hospital she had founded in Calcutta in 1934.

The Russian space authorities have opened a permanent post office on their *Mir* space station.

Until 1874, all British pillar boxes were painted a dull bronze green.

The Royal Mail has its own miniature underground railway system, which runs under London from Whitechapel in the east to Paddington in the west, with intermediate stops where mail is added to the train in small sealed containers. An average of 35,000 bags of mail are handled daily and the journey across the city takes 26 minutes.

Late deliveries always make the news, like the picture postcard from Seaton in Devon which, according to *The Times*, was delivered, 55 years after it was sent, to a hospital that had closed in 1988.

Nor is this problem unique to the British post. Associated Press reports that it took Polish postmen seven years to deliver a Christmas card 20 miles (32 kms) from Opole to Strzelce Opolskie, and that it took 10 years for an airmail letter to travel from Buenos Aires to Verona in Italy. Both the sender and the addressee had died in the meantime.

Agence France Press reported in May 1989 that a postcard sent by a German POW to his wife from Moscow in 1945 was delivered almost 44 years later, on the couple's 50th wedding anniversary.

BLINDNESS

Hank Dekker was 42 and had been blind for 11 years when he became the first blind person to sail alone across the Pacific, from San Francisco to Hawaii, in 1983. He spent 24 days travelling the 3,376 miles (5,400 kms) in his 25-foot (7.6-metre) sloop *Dark Star*. He used braille charts and compass, a talking clock, and a computer navigation system that read his position aloud. His long-range radio failed after three days and he was out of contact for three weeks.

Peter Wood is one of Britain's only blind drivers, relying on his navigator using simple terms used in rally driving – to me, to you – to guide him. As a fund-raising stunt, he drove the length of Great Britain from Land's End to John O'Groats, a distance of 873 miles (1,405 kms), in a specially constructed rough-terrain vehicle through forests, over farm lands, bogs and beaches. He was not allowed to use public highways.

The world speed record for a car driven by a blind person was set by Mike Landsell of Ascot, Berkshire when he reached 130.97 mph (210 km/h) in a Ford Sierra Cosworth in November 1991.

In 1992, 63 contestants took part in Calcutta's Third Annual Car Rally for the Blind, a hazardous 50-mile (80-km) race through one of the most congested cities on Earth. In this unique event, sighted drivers are teamed with blind navigators working from braille directions. The main hazard turned out to be dust settling on the braille sheets but, despite this difficulty, all but one of the rally cars crossed the finishing line.

The Rally is organized by India's National Association for the Blind, which stages the event to prove that the sightless should be given the chance of a job. West Bengal has more than a million blind people; only 70 have so far been employed by government and industry.

In June 1980 Edwin Robinson of Falmouth, Maine, who had been blinded nine years earlier following a road accident, had his sight restored after being struck by lightning as he sheltered under a tree. He could also hear without his hearing aid, which broke when he fell.

Gun Thoresson regained her sight in 1983 after 23 years of blindness, when her Swedish dentist removed several decaying molars. Swedish doctors now believe that her blindness was caused by the metal fillings, but dentists are said to be sceptical of such claims.

Tyre-fitter Kevin Willis had been blind for a year when he suddenly regained his sight in 1983. His wife threw a bucket of water over him while he was playing with his kids in a paddling-pool. The plastic bucket tapped his head at just the right point. His wife Karen told reporters: 'The doctor was amazed when I told him Kevin had regained his sight. I have always joked that all he needed was a good clout on the head.'

Ellen Head was 84 and had been 90 per cent blind for three years, when an earthquake shook her flat in Newcastle, 100 miles (160 kms) north of Sydney, Australia, for five seconds in December 1989. As a result, she regained her sight.

In 1984 Japan became the first country to print banknotes with raised lettering for blind people.

The world's first talking traffic lights were installed in Benidorm, Spain in 1989. They tell pedestrians, in English, French, Spanish and German, when it is safe to cross.

131

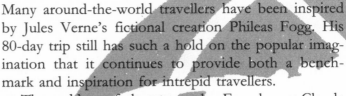

Many around-the-world travellers have been inspired by Jules Verne's fictional creation Phileas Fogg. His 80-day trip still has such a hold on the popular imagination that it continues to provide both a benchmark and inspiration for intrepid travellers.

The saddest of these was the Frenchman Claude Mosse who, having successfully survived a train crash, a typhoon and a robbery, arrived back at London's Reform Club on 7 September 1977, with five hours to spare, having used nothing but surface transport, only to be refused entry because the club had 'blackballed' him in his absence, claiming his adventure was a publicity stunt. The 50-year-old journalist won his own weight in whisky – about eight cases – from a whisky company for completing the challenge.

Verne was inspired by the 1872 tour undertaken by Thomas Cook, founder of the travel firm, whose journey was designed to drum up business, and he drew heavily from Cook's correspondence with *The Times*. Cook took 222 days to complete his east-to-west journey (Fogg went west-to-east) but was only physically travelling on about 90 of them.

Experts who have studied 1872 travel timetables estimate that 88 days would have been Fogg's minimum time. In 1987, the *Sunday Times* commissioned Thomas Cook and Lloyd's maritime information service to work out whether Fogg's journey could be achieved in modern times. They estimated the minimum time now needed would be 102 days.

Dave Kunst walked around the world in four and a half years, covering a distance of 15,000 miles (24,140 kms) and wearing out 21 pairs of shoes. He was seriously wounded when his brother John was shot to death by Afghan bandits 30 months into the journey. Dave returned to the US to recuperate and then, undeterred, set off again from Afghanistan with Peter, his younger brother – accompanied by 40 armed Afghan government guards.

Unable to get permission to cross China by foot, the brothers took a ship to Australia where they walked across that continent – equal to the distance across China. The final leg of the journey was from Newport Beach, California, to Waseca, Minnesota, where Dave arrived on 5 October 1974.

Rick Hansen was 29 when he arrived back in Vancouver in May 1987, having travelled 25,000 miles (40,250 kms) in a 26-month journey around the world in a wheelchair, during which he raised over £6 million ($8.5m) on behalf of the disabled.

On 13 March 1988, John Sanders arrived back in Fremantle, Western Australia, having become the first person to circumnavigate the world three times non-stop. The voyage, in his 46-foot (14-metre) sloop *Parry Endeavour*, took him 658 days, covering a distance of 80,000 nautical miles.

John Foster Frazer, a professional journalist, set off to bicycle around the world in July 1896 with two friends, Edward Lunn and F.H. Lowe. Over the next two years and two months they cycled 19,237 miles (31,100 kms) through 17 countries and across three continents, an adventure Frazer chronicled in his book *Round the World on a Wheel*.

Many cyclists since have emulated this feat. In 1976 Robert Morris arrived back in Randolph Township, New Jersey, having pedalled 30,500 miles (49,000 kms) across 30 nations in 27 months; while Steve Williams, Peter Wuerslin and Tim Young from Jackson, Wyoming, left home on 25 October 1980, and spent the next six and a half years travelling 45,000 miles (72,500 kms) through 45 countries and six continents on their customized 15-speed bikes.

Perhaps the strangest of all world travellers was Harry Bensley who, in 1908, accepted a wager of £21,000 ($30,000) that he could not walk round the world without revealing his identity. Disguised in a metal helmet, the 'masked walker' set off, with a 'minder' appointed by the National Sporting Club and his belongings in a pram. His other challenge was that he had to marry before his journey was complete.

He had almost finished his walk in 1914 when war broke out and he returned to England to enlist. Although he lost his wager, he was awarded a £4,000 ($6,000) prize for effort.

FUNGI

There are believed to be about 100,000 species of fungi. Less than half of them are mushrooms: the rest are lichens, yeasts and moulds. An estimated 2,000 species are edible, of which 100 are specially favoured. Britons eat about 75,000 tonnes of mushrooms a year, but nearly all are of one sort, *Agaricus bisporus.*

The Little People of Irish folklore may have sprung from hallucinations engendered by the consumption of 'magic mushrooms' *(Psilocybe semilanceata)*, eaten in stone-built sweathouses, a traditional structure that has now virtually disappeared in Ireland, according to Irish historian Anthony Weir.

'Fairy rings' are caused by fungus growing outwards in circular patterns from an initial spore, and erupting in a ring of mushrooms and toadstools. It appears that in the process it accumulates potassium, which explains why it leaves sickly-looking grass in the centre, deprived of this vital nutrient, and brightens the grass at the edge of the circle.

R. Gordon Wasson was vice-president of the giant US firm Morgan Guaranty Trust. While holding down the job of head of its international banking division, he travelled in 1955 to a Mexican village where he and his wife became the first whites in history to be administered the psilocybin 'magic' mushroom in an ancient Indian religious ceremony.

Wasson and his Russian-born wife, Valentina, had previously spent 30 years documenting the use of mushrooms in the early history of spirituality. Wasson had been alerted to the continued existence of the Mexican mushroom ceremony by Robert Graves.

Wasson retired from the bank in 1964 and, together with Dr Albert Hoffman, the man who discovered LSD in the 1940s, returned to Mexico to test synthetic psilocybin pills. When he died in December 1986, he was remembered by friends at the bank as one of the 'big men of banking', a writer of 'eloquent and colourful memoranda'. Film-maker Philip Black described him as 'the perfect old-fashioned gentleman with an extraordinary twinkle in his eye'.

It was announced in 1992 that the biggest living thing on Earth is now known to be a giant mushroom fungus. This startling fact was discovered by James Anderson, Professor of Botany at the University of Toronto, and his student Myron Smith.

They confirmed this after four years of study, using genetic analysis techniques to establish that samples of the underground fungus taken from various plots in a Michigan forest — over an area of at least 37 acres (15 hectares), larger than 20 football pitches — was in fact the same individual. It is estimated to weigh some 10 tonnes and to be 1,500 years old.

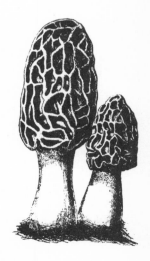

The Michigan fungus (*Armillaria bulbosa*) is known

to gourmets as the honey mushroom, to gardeners as the shoe-string root.. Mushrooms are just the fruiting bodies of the fungus; the bulk of it lies below ground as a network of intertwining filaments known as the fungal thallus.

One month after this fungus was first described in scientific literature, it was dwarfed by news of another champion fungus from Washington State which is 40 times larger.

The tentacles of this fine example of the underground honey or shoestring fungus *(Armillaria ostoyae)* spread over 1,500 acres (600 hectares) and it is believed to be between 500 and 1,000 years old. Its discoverers have made no attempt to guess its weight.

Even this record is open to question, according to a *New Scientist* correspondent.. Amongst other record-holders with a claim to being called the biggest living thing on Earth, he cites an aspen *(Populus fremaloides)* that covers 200 acres (81 hectares) and is over 10,000 years old.

There has been a massive decline in both the number of mushroom species and the abundance of those species that have survived, right across northern and central Europe. Over-collecting is a minor threat in this regard. Habitat loss is certainly an important factor but the main culprit is air pollution, in particular acid rain.

Why should this be the case? It is because the underground part of the fungus lives in close relationship to the roots of trees, increasing the amount of nitrogen – an essential plant nutrient – available to them. Mycologists believe that the roots might be rejecting the fungi because they are now receiving a surfeit of nitrogen in acid rain. Each hectare of Dutch forest, for instance, is reckoned to have 130 lbs (60 kgs) of nitrogen oxides falling on it each year. The problem may be compounded by the drift from nitrogen-rich fertilizer sprayed on farmland.

Foresters in Hiroshima have been using the US *Landsat V* satellite to help pinpoint areas in which the *matsutake* fungus can be found. This plump-stemmed mushroom is a gourmet favourite, costing up to £60 ($85) a piece in Japanese stores, and is so expensive that the average Japanese can only afford to eat it on special occasions.

It is also very hard to locate as it only grows on red-pine trees that are alive but declining. Picking out these trees from healthy ones is something that satellite imagery, using a range of frequencies of light, is very good at.

By correlating this data with the known conditions that *matsutake* need for growth, the Hiroshima researchers hope they can pinpoint this elusive, élitist fungus.

DEATH

Thanatology is the study of the social and psychological dimensions of dying, death and bereavement.

Between 1832 and 1932, the poor who died in institutions in Britain provided all but half of one per cent of the bodies dissected in London's anatomy schools – a total of 57,000 corpses.

Sleepy Hollow Cemetery in Concord, Massachusetts, which contains the graves of Thoreau and Emerson amongst others, also contains the  unusual tombstone of Sheila Shea, who died of cancer in 1986. At her request, the inscription reads, 'Who the hell is Sheila Shea?'

In July 1986, Mrs Jean McManus of Seaton Carew, Cleveland, died in hospital of tetanus. She had contracted it after impaling her leg on a fishing rod held by her garden gnome.

In 1987 the Liberal life peer Lord Avebury expressed his wish that after his death his body be bequeathed to the kitchens at Battersea Dogs' Home 'to give the doggies a good meal'.

A total of 55 million people died in the Second World War, of whom 20 million were soldiers. It was revealed in Britain only in 1982 that, under the War Dead Act, passed by Congress in 1946, every American next of kin had the right to ask for the return of their dead. As a result the US had spent $164 million on repatriating 170,000 bodies, of which 6,000 came from Britain. The British authorities kept this secret because they could not afford to do the same.

On 22 May 1989, Danie du Toit, a South African businessman, choked to death on a peppermint, minutes after making a speech at a club meeting warning that death could come at any time and one must live for the moment.

In January 1986, an Indonesian MP died in Jakarta on his way home after winning a two-day battle in the regional Assembly to secure funds for his local city hospital to buy a hearse.

On 25 November 1986, in Towson, Maryland, an actress collapsed and died on stage during a production of *The Drunkard*. It occurred during her character's death scene, right after singing *Please Don't Talk About Me When I'm Gone*.

A poodle called Cachi died when it fell from a balcony in Buenos Aires on 23 October 1988. It also killed three people in the process: Señora Marta Espina died when the dog fell on her head; Señora Edith Sola, a witness to this unusual fatality, died when she was knocked down by a bus; and an unidentified bystander, who witnessed both deaths, had a heart attack and died on the way to hospital.

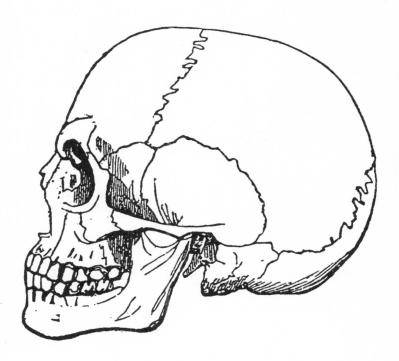

Choking is now the sixth most common form of accidental death in the United States, according to the National Safety Council. Steak, lobster tails, hard-boiled eggs and bread get fatally stuck in some 2,500 throats every year. Choking is more lethal than lightning, snakebites, air crashes, and even gun mishaps. In 40 per cent of these deaths, when food 'goes down the wrong way', the food is either a hot dog or candy.

CORIOLIS EFFECT

All things that move over the face of the Earth tend to sidle from their appointed paths – to the right in the Northern Hemisphere, and to the left in the Southern Hemisphere. This tendency was first analysed in detail by the nineteenth-century French mathematician G.G. Coriolis and is due simply to the Earth's rotation.

Few people realize that as they drive down the road at 60 mph (100 km/h), they would drift off it at the rate of 15 feet per mile (4.6 metres per 1.6 kms) if it wasn't for the frictional resistance of the tyres to any lateral motion.

In the First World War, the giant German gun nicknamed Big Bertha was used to bombard Paris from a site 70 miles (113 kms) away. The shells took three minutes to reach their target and the gunners had to take into account the Coriolis drift to the right, which over that distance amounted to a full mile (1.6 kms).

The Coriolis effect is 50 per cent stronger at the poles: on frictionless ice, a person walking at 4 mph (6.4 km/h) would drift 250 feet (76 metres) off a straight path at the end of a mile, which explains the wanderings of lost polar explorers.

It also has a major effect on the weather. If it were not for the Coriolis effect, the winds would rush directly from high-pressure to low-pressure areas, without allowing any strong 'highs' or 'lows' to develop.

There would be no opportunity for cyclones or anti-cyclones to develop and so our weather would be much less changeable than it is. This is the situation in the Tropics, where the Coriolis effect is zero, smoothing out atmospheric differences and earning the region the name of 'the doldrums'.

QUAGGA

The last known quagga *(Equus burchelli quagga)* died in Amsterdam Zoo in 1883.

A sub-species of the zebra family, the quagga was named in imitation of the animal's shrill, neighing cry. It was mainly brown in colour with white legs and tail and a striped head and neck. Geographically restricted to certain areas of the South African veldt, huge herds of these animals were shot for food and hides by the Boer settlers. Their lightweight skins were made into sturdy sacks for storage and transportation.

Quaggas were also captured and semi-domesticated for use as 'watchdogs'.

In England in the 1830s there was a vogue for using quaggas as harness animals. London Zoo tried to breed them in the 1860s but their one highly-strung stallion beat itself to death against the walls of its enclosure.

The quagga was wiped out in a little over 30 years, the last wild one being shot in 1878. However, a group of South African researchers is currently attempting to 'retrieve' it from oblivion.

Analysis of DNA from preserved samples of quagga tissue has confirmed that it was not a species in its own right but was closely related genetically to the plains zebra.

Breeding experiments with a small herd of these living relatives, designed to enhance their quagga-like characteristics, have already produced eight foals since October 1988. One foal in particular, born in 1992, bears an uncanny likeness to its long-lost relative.

The world's foremost exponents of forensic climatology are the staff of Environment Canada, who operate the Ontario Weather Service. Dave Murdoch has become the world's first recognized expert in his field and has given evidence in more than 400 cases in criminal and civil courts, in Canada and the US.

They solved the rain-hat murder case, in which a woman's body was found lying on dry ground in a Toronto park. In her purse was a plastic rain-hat that was still damp. Radar records of precipitation showed only two areas around the city where it had been raining at the time of death. Investigations in these areas led to an arrest within hours.

The first person to be recorded as having used entomology in forensic science was a Frenchman, Dr Bergeret, who in 1850 conducted an autopsy on the body of a child found by a plasterer while repairing a broken mantelpiece. He found that the flesh fly *(Sarcophaga carnaria)* had deposited larvae on the body during 1848 and concluded that the murderer had occupied the house during that year.

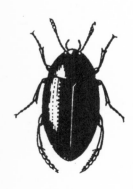

Forensic entomology was placed on a firm scientific footing by P. Megnin, whose 1894 work *La Faune des Cadavres: Application de l'Entomologie à la Médecine Légale* argued that, as the body decays, different species of insects will be attracted to it at different stages of decomposition, and thus identifying the species will fix the time of death. This has proved to be correct in theory, but in practice there are so many factors involved that each case has to be taken on its merits.

Britain's only full-time forensic entomologist is Dr Zak Erzinclioglu of the Zoological Department at Cambridge University, who is consulted by detectives about once a month. In one case, involving the mummified corpse of a woman, he discovered that it was infested with the larva of a small moth and, from the existence of its maggot cases, estimated the corpse was three years old. At first he could not determine the time of year of death but he then found empty maggot cases of a blowfly *(Phormia terraenovae)*, a rare species active early in the summer. This led him to predict the time of death as May, which was subsequently borne out by other evidence and led to the conviction of the murdered woman's husband.

Roxie C. Laybourne is a feather expert at the Smithsonian Institution's National Museum of Natural History and is often called to give forensic evidence.

She recalls: 'One time I had a Colorado case. A girl had been killed, and a guy – the suspect – was in jail. He wore a necklace made with the foot of a great horned owl. The girl had marks on her that the police thought could have been made by the owl foot; and they also found a feather. I ID'd it. It wasn't an owl feather; it was a chicken. I think he was released; I felt good about it.'

Mrs Laybourne, who has written the standard work on feather identification, uses two key means to match often fragmentary evidence to the right bird species – the gross structure of the feather and its position on the bird's body, and its microscopic cellular structure.

She has the advantage of having access to the huge Smithsonian collection, which includes 421,000 stuffed birds and more than 21,000 birds preserved in alcohol in the 'Spirit Room'; the museum also holds 32,000 bird skeletons, 39,000 nests and 96,000 eggs.

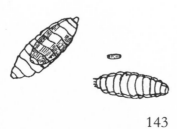

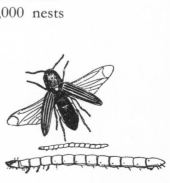

As she lay in a coma in a New Jersey nursing home, Karen Ann Quinlan triggered an historic battle. Her religious parents argued that she should not be kept alive artificially but should be allowed to die, and in 1976 the New Jersey Supreme Court agreed. All her life support systems, except for a feeding tube in her nose, were switched off. But instead of passing away within hours, she survived a further nine years. She died on 12 July 1985, at the age of 31.

The longest coma victim was an American woman who never regained consciousness after an appendix operation she had as a child and who died in either 1974 or 1978 after lying unconscious for 34 or 38 years (sources vary).

Another famous case was that of Major Reginald Bristow, who went into a coma in March 1959 when he suffered serious head injuries in a road crash in Scotland. He eventually died on 6 June 1977, in a hospital at Elgin, Grampian, at the age of 66. He was shaved daily, had his hair cut regularly, was turned twice a day to prevent bed sores and was fed intravenously. According to a spokesman for the Grampian Health Board, 'His appearance when he died was apparently exactly the same as when he had the accident. He was described as being in a state of suspended animation.' He never saw the youngest of his three sons, Anthony, who was born two months after the accident.

In 1986, at China's Shijiazhuang Air Force Hospital, 12-year-old Xie Xiaoli awoke from an 11-year sleep. She had fallen from her bed at the age of one, injuring her neck.

DEMOLITION

In 1975, a team of 40 karate experts demolished 12 terraced houses at Poolsbrook, near Chesterfield in England, using only their heads, hands and feet. It was a charity stunt.

In 1980, another team of karate experts demolished Nos 120–136, Kilton Road, Worksop, Nottinghamshire, in similar fashion in 14 hours.

The motto of the US-based firm of Controlled Demolition Inc., owned and run by the Loiseaux family for more than 50 years, is 'Fragmentation at a Price'.

DEMOLITION DERBY

This destructive form of entertainment was invented in 1958 by Larry Mendelsohn, a part-time stock car driver, who noticed that people were more interested in crashes than races.

He bought a run-down circuit called Islip Raceway and recruited drivers willing to smash into each other using a newspaper ad that read, 'Wanted: 100 Men not Afraid to Die.'

The idea was a huge success and became a regular feature on ABC's *Wide World of Sports*, achieving an audience of 25 million viewers by 1974.

A number of imitations resulted, including Blackout Demolition (the winner is the last car with its lights left shining), Football Demolition (which uses a small car as a ball) and Figure 8 Racing (in which cars criss-cross in a 50 mph (80 km/h) game of chicken).

The modern image of Santa Claus as a cheery and rotund figure who arrives on rooftops in a sleigh drawn by reindeer and climbs down the chimney derived from an 1823 poem, published anonymously by Professor Clement Clark Moore, entitled 'A Visit from St Nicholas'. An 1836 drawing by Thomas Nast, an American of Bavarian descent, entitled *The Coming of Santa Claus*, gave him his name – an Americanization of the Dutch *Sinter Klaas* – and established his uniform of hat, tunic and boots.

But Moore's influence may lie much deeper, as he was a scholar of Hebrew and Oriental language, and had a particular interest in the shamanistic tribes of north-east Siberia – the 'reindeer people'. The shamans mediated between the great Reindeer Spirit and mortals by eating fly agaric, a red and white hallucinogenic mushroom that gives flying sensations. These peoples – the Koryak, Chuckee and Kamchadel – live in *yurts,* in which the smokehole is the main entrance. Is it coincidence that, in Germany, the fly agaric mushroom is considered the patron plant of chimney sweeps?

The town of Santa Claus, Indiana, had a college for department store Santas, who can graduate with a B.Sc. (Bachelor of Santa Clausing).

Letters addressed to Santa Claus, Greenland, will get through, thanks to an international postal agreement. They are funnelled via the Danish Post Office to the Copenhagen HQ of the Greenland Post Office, where envelopes containing a letter from Santa and a small gift are addressed before being air-freighted to Post Station 3910 at Søndre Strømfjord, in Greenland. Here stamps and stickers plus a local postmark are added and the letters are sent air mail all over the world. This service was originally instigated in the 1930s by the Royal Greenland Trade Depart-ment; it now handles 5,000 letters a year.

In 1962, a tradition of writing to Santa Claus began when a journalist reported that a six-year-old girl had written to him at Himmelpforten, a West German town whose name means 'Heaven's Gates' – and got a reply, written by the local postman. The town now has a full-time Santa who receives 15,000 letters annually.

In 1980 a woman from Peterborough threatened to invoke the Equal Opportunities Act against her local Job Centre for refusing to accept her application for the job of Father Christmas.

In Spain, children traditionally receive their presents on 6 January, known as El Dia de los Reyes – the Day of the Kings. The night before (Twelfth Night), children leave a pair of shoes at the window to let the Three Kings – Gaspar, Melchior and Balthasar – know there are children in the house. This is in addition to celebrations on 24 December for Papa Noël.

Two physicists at the University of Chicago named Gary Horowitz and Basilis Xanthopoulos have worked out how it is possible for Santa Claus to visit every home in the world on a single night. The Earth's rotation gives Santa 24 hours of night to visit the world's two billion households and to cover 100 million miles (160m kms). This means that his reindeer carry him at 70,000 miles (112,650 kms) per second and that he spends just one half of one ten-thousandth of a second at each home. That's why you never see him – he's moving too fast.

In 1978 the Inter-City Oil Company in Duluth, Minnesota, began making out its Xmas cards to its 15,000 customers in May, in order to beat an increase in postal charges. The message on the envelope read: 'Who's the nut sending Xmas cards this time of year?'

In Russia, Father Christmas is known as Grandfather Frost; he is invariably accompanied by a Snow Maiden.

The carol *Once in Royal David's City* is in fact a poem written by Mrs C.F. Alexander, a 25-year-old Ulster Sunday school teacher, as part of a sequence of hymns written to illustrate the Apostles' Creed. It also included *All Things Bright and Beautiful* and *There is a Green Hill Far Away*.

In February 1983 Associated Press reported that a man in a red cloak visited the hamlet of Merry Christmas in Texas (which has a population of ten), but instead of bringing gifts he stole $500.

According to Dr Odd Halvorsen, a professor in the Department of Ecology at Tromsø University in Norway, Rudolf the reindeer's red nose was probably caused by a parasitic infection of its respiratory system. Reindeer are prey to a wide variety of parasites and blood-sucking insects; more than 25 different species of worms live in their stomachs alone. Over 2,000 worms have been recovered from a single reindeer's stomach.

Another scientist from Tromsø, Arne Fjellberg, revealed that the average Christmas tree contains about 30,000 bugs and insects, including midges, fleas, spiders, beetles, lice and parasitic wasps. Most of them die within a few days.

The traditional Christmas cracker was either invented by Tom Smith, a London baker and confectioner, or by James Hovell, another London confectioner, between 1840 and 1860. Each man gave his name to a firm of cracker manufacturers, both of which survived intact until 1985, when Hovells swallowed Smith's to form a new company which now controls 45 per cent of the market, producing 50 million crackers a year, worth around £7 million ($10m).

The most valuable Christmas card ever was probably that sent by the Gaekwar of Baroda to an Englishwoman of his affections. Made of ivory and decorated with 44 diamonds, it took six months to make, and was valued at £500,000 ($710,000) in 1903.

A CHRISTMAS "CARD"

The Witchita-based Nieman-Marcus department store chain specializes in supplying sumptious, decadent and unusual Christmas presents – a tradition they began in 1965, when an eccentric millionaire from Denton, Texas, asked them if they could have his Labrador retriever zinc-plated. Since then they have sold a Lamborghini carved out of Gouda cheese, a visit from a team of silver-clad midget 'extraterrestrials' who repaint all the horizontal surfaces in your home, the abandoned sidings of the Rock Island Railroad and twin nuclear-fuel reprocessing plants.

KIDOLOGY

A Spaniard known as the King of Kidology invented 3,000 children for himself over a period of eight years in the 1970s, and extracted 30 million francs ($5.3m) from the French social security system. He then successfully evaded the authorities and went to live in his native town of Valencia in Spain, from which he could not be extradited.

In 1980 a woman from California was accused of a massive welfare fraud, in which it was claimed she collected £150,000 ($213,000) in benefits for more than 40 children over a seven-year period, and a further £50,000 ($71,000) in food stamps and other benefits. She owned two mansions, 120 apartments and many luxury cars. She had ten children of her own.

A Belgian adopted 30,903 children at a refugee camp in Somalia in April 1981 and then returned to his native country and tried to arrange family allowance for them – a total of 1,500 million Belgian francs ($44m) a year. He had the notion while recuperating from an accident in which his car had collided with a camel.

POLYTHENE

Polythene was first discovered at ICI by Eric Fawcett and Reginald Gibson on 24 March 1933, when a failed experiment to react ethylene with benzaldehyde under pressure of 1,900 atmospheres produced half a gram of a new 'waxy solid' in the pressure vessel.

It was several years before this new polymer could be consistently produced. No one could envisage a use for it until another chemist in the corporation noticed its similarity to gutta percha, the material used to sheathe submarine telephone cables. Tests showed that polythene would do the job better. One hundred tonnes were ordered as a result, making it feasible for ICI to build the first production plant, which came on-stream the day that Hitler invaded Poland.

One problem was that unless the production unit was shut down for two weeks every two or three years, it exploded. ICI initially decided to proceed on this basis, until one year when the warning came too late and the plant blew up. It was rebuilt out of pre-fabricated units, which ICI found was cheaper than losing two weeks' production. From then on the plant was allowed to explode, and was rebuilt around the concrete skeleton. An explosion-proof plant was not built until 1978.

HUMAN HEDGEHOG

Pensioner Jens Kjaer Jenslon has become known as 'the human hedgehog' in his native Denmark, and his agonizing problems have secured him a place in medical history.

In 1971 Jens, then 57, was cutting his hedge of spiky barberry bushes. He piled the cut branches in a heap, tripped, fell on them, and was pierced by thousands of inch-long (2.5-cm) thorns.

He spent the next six months in hospital having 6,000 thorns removed. But still more deeply embedded thorns kept working their way out, and over the next six years Jens returned to the hospital 248 times.

He has now had a total of 32,131 thorns removed – not counting those he has pulled out at home.

Frankincense, a French word meaning 'pure incense', is mainly derived from the bitter, milky-white resin of a low, spiky tree, *Boswellia carteri*, found in the dry highlands of the Arabian peninsula and Somalia. Like rubber, the resin is extracted by scraping the bark and collecting it several months later.

Myrrh is a reddish resin obtained from a number of species of *Commiphora*, short and thorny trees found across Ethiopia and Kenya as well as in the same regions as frankincense.

The trees produce the resin as a temporary dressing for damaged bark. In modern times it is collected by nomadic peoples and sold to governmental agencies, but on a smaller level than in ancient times. Both have been extensively used in medicine.

The ancient Egyptians used both resins in the mummification process. The Hebrews mixed myrrh with wine as an anaesthetic for a condemned man – the drink offered to Jesus Christ at the Crucifixion. The Royal Navy used it on a large scale for treating scurvy. The Victorians used a tincture of myrrh and borax as a toothpaste. Myrrh is still used today as an ingredient in throat pastilles and cough mixtures.

One of the major suppliers of incense to the world market, and the only producer in the UK, are the 40 monks of Prinknash Abbey in the Cotswolds.

Here frankincense is blended with other hardened gum resins and oils from rosewood or bay until it is turned into what looks like large brown sugar crystals. It is sold in tins under five brand names – Basilica, Cathedral, Abbey, Sanctuary and Priory – and is designed to be burnt in a thurible or censer filled with quick-lighting charcoal.

When Kazumi Kimata had his right arm severed below the elbow in an industrial accident at a small factory near Nagoya, Japan, doctors told him they couldn't rejoin it. So he took it home, put it in a plastic bag, prayed over it, and buried it in a grave in his garden. Six hours later another surgeon offered to try to graft the arm back on, so Mr Kimata disinterred his arm, took it to the hospital, and underwent a 12-hour operation. His arm is now working fine.

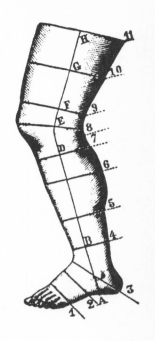

In December 1976, a circus trainer in Sydney had his right thumb sown back on after it had been bitten off by a runaway zebra.

In 1977, a student at Clemson University in Atlanta, Georgia, underwent a successful seven-hour operation to reattach his penis after he had been attacked by a man whose estranged wife he had been dating. Such a reimplantation had only been performed successfully three times before up to that date.

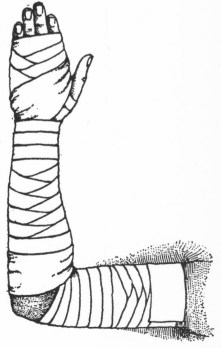

In January 1978, Las Vegas doctors sewed back the hand of a 21-year-old woman who had chopped it off with a machete after 'sinning against God'. She arrived at the hospital quoting the Gospel according to St Matthew: 'Wherefore if thy hand or thy foot offend thee, cut them off and cast them from thee.'

In 1989, ten-year-old Timothy Mathias survived a five-hour operation at St Joseph's Hospital and Medical Center in Phoenix, Arizona, to have his skull reattached to his spine after an accident on his bike, in which his head was almost severed from his body.

Einstein was a late developer, and even at the age of nine he could not speak fluently. His parents feared that he might be subnormal, and it is probable that in early childhood he suffered from dyslexia, or word-blindness.

In her biography of her brother, the late Maja Winteler-Einstein recorded that he had a terrible temper, which caused his whole face, except for the tip of his nose, to turn yellow. He threw a chair at his violin teacher and a bowling ball at his sister. On another occasion, he threatened to 'knock a hole' in Maja's head with a toy trowel.

On Christmas Eve 1928, Einstein and the eminent physicist Leo Szilard filed a patent in England for a refrigerator. Their researches had been inspired by reports of a family in Berlin who had been killed by poisonous fumes leaking from their fridge. A prototype was built but proved too noisy for domestic use – but the magnetic pump at the heart of many nuclear reactors is based on their noisy fridge.

After his move to America, Einstein and Gustav Bucky patented a 'light intensity self-adjusting camera' – in many respects the forerunner of modern automatic exposure-control cameras.

In 1952, Einstein was invited to be President of Israel after the death of Chaim Weizmann but he refused, saying, 'I know a little about nature but hardly anything about men.'

At his own request, Einstein's brain was removed for posthumous study at an autopsy after his death on 18 April 1955. Placed in a formaldehyde-filled jar, it was driven to Philadelphia where it was sectioned in a lab at the University of Pennsylvania. Studies progressed slowly and the brain was forgotten until a reporter for the *New Jersey Monthly* went in search of it in August 1978. He found bits of it, including the cerebellum, in mason jars in a cardboard box on a shelf in a lab in Wichita, Kansas.

The original manuscript of Einstein's *Compatibility of the Field Equation in the Unified Field Theory* was auctioned on 25 June 1980, after coming to light in a curious fashion.

The Brooklyn Jewish Centre in the city had decided to investigate the contents of an ancient safe in their cellar and, as the combination had been lost and a professional cracksman was required, they offered the large and valuable safe as scrap metal to whoever could open it. The manuscript was found safely inside; records showed that Einstein had presented it at a dinner in 1934.

The first draft of Einstein's August 1939 letter to President Roosevelt, which explained the theoretical possibility of making an atomic bomb and urged the USA to develop one, was sold at auction at Christie's in New York in December 1986 for $220,000 – the highest price paid for a twentieth-century letter – to the millionaire Malcolm Forbes, who died in 1990.

Forbes also owned the log of the US pilot who dropped the bomb on Hiroshima. Einstein called the letter 'the one great mistake in my life'.

The first film that Einstein ever saw was Eisenstein's *Battleship Potemkin*, on 3 June 1930.

In 1990 a small number of scholars claimed that much of Einstein's early work, including perhaps the theory of relativity, should have been credited to his first wife. At the very least, they claim, she should get a co-author credit.

One letter from Einstein, written to his wife in 1901, reads: 'How happy and proud I will be when the two of us together will have brought our work on the relative motion [the theory of relativity] to a victorious conclusion.'

Serbian Mileva Maric was 21 when she entered the Swiss Federal Institute of Technology in Zurich, where she met the 17-year-old Einstein. They became lovers and had an illegitimate daughter in 1902, who subsequently disappeared, and may still be alive somewhere.

They later married and had two sons, but as Einstein's fame grew, Mileva – by most accounts a brilliant mathematician in her own right – became lost in his shadow. They separated in 1914, and eventually divorced, Mileva receiving his Nobel Prize money as alimony three years later. Einstein remarried, this time to his cousin Elsa Einstein, and moved to America, leaving Mileva and the children alone. One son died in a mental institution, the other became an engineering professor. Mileva died in 1948. She never published a scientific paper under her own name.

PRODUCTS

Bag Balm comes in a bright green can, decorated with clover blossoms and a portrait of a cow, and was designed to heal the chapped udders of dairy cattle. However, so many other uses have been found for it since its introduction in 1908 that this yellow goo has become legendary.

It is used by skiers as protection against windburn and by marathon runners to prevent blisters; it can also prevent acne and haemorrhoids, users claim. Others employ it for removing rust, and it was a favoured lubricant for the 105-mm howitzer in the Vietnam War. It can be used to waterproof boots and has even had a golf tournament named after it – the Bag Balm Invitational, held annually at the Cedar

Crest Golf Course in Marysville, Washington. The grand prize is a 10-ounce (283-gm) can of Bag Balm, worth $2.75.

Made in Lyndonville, Vermont by the Dairy Association Company, Bag Balm is a combination of four ingredients: lanolin and petroleum jelly (moisturizing agents), an antiseptic called 8 Hydroxyquinoline sulfate and pine oil.

Products at the 1987 Fad Fair in New York in November 1987 included a Dobermask (a mask of a Dobermann pinscher designed to slip over the head of a cat or puppy to deter burglars) and Everbrown (an already-dead plant that takes the guilt out of watching your plants die).

The Swiss Army knife is produced by two companies in Switzerland – Wenger and Victorinox – and every new Swiss soldier (40,000 recruits a year) is supplied with one, with four blades and a silver-coloured handle.

When he was in office, President Johnson ordered 4,000 with his signature inlaid on the handle and in 1978 NASA ordered 50 of the master craftsmen models for the crews of the space shuttle. The *U-2* pilot Gary Powers had one on him when he was shot down over the Soviet Union in 1960. Some 15 million of these miniature tool boxes are sold annually around the world. A Victorinox knife is described as 'original', a Wenger knife as 'genuine'.

HAPPY BIRTHDAY

Happy Birthday to You is based on a melody composed in 1893 by two teachers from Kentucky, Patty Smith Hill and her sister Mildred. The lyrics were added later and it was copyrighted in 1935. In 1988, after passing through the hands of many music publishing companies, it was bought by Warner Communications Inc., who will be entitled to royalties from the song until 2010 when copyright expires. In theory every public performance of the song should require paying a fee to the company; in practice this would be both undesirable and unenforceable. The previous owners, Birchtree Ltd, confined their copyright enforcement activities to companies that recorded the song for sale or used it in theatrical or film productions. Royalties amounted to a modest £560,000 ($800,000) a year.

ZONULES OF ZINN

First named by J. G. Zinn in his *Descriptio Anatomica Oculi Humani*, published in Göttingen in 1755, his zonules are to be found in the eye. Consisting of three clear cellophane-like circles, they hold the lens suspended in the centre of the circle of ciliary muscles that control the focusing of vision.

As the eye focuses on a nearby object, the circle of ciliary muscles contracts, reducing the tension on the zonules of Zinn and allowing the lens to fatten as it returns to its natural, more spherical shape. When the eye is focused on infinity, the ciliary muscles are most relaxed, putting the zonules of Zinn under maximum tension so that they pull the lens flat.

TRANSSEXUAL

The first person to undergo a sex change operation was in the US armed forces. George Jorgenson, Jr went to Denmark and underwent almost 2,000 hormone injections and many surgical operations under the supervision of Danish hormone expert Dr Christian Hamburger before being transformed into Christine Jorgenson. The story hit the press on 2 December 1952, and she was able to earn a living subsequently from sales of her autobiography, a nightclub act (theme song: *I Enjoy Being A Girl*), stage roles, and appearances on TV and the college lecture circuit. George/Christine died on 3 May 1989 of bladder cancer.

The French Foreign Legion dates from 1831, and was formed by King Louis-Philippe, who believed such a force would help absorb many of the political refugees in France. He also planned for them to be sent to fight the colonial war in Algeria, thus freeing the regular army to protect his flimsy hold on the monarchy at home. By all accounts the first battalion was a disaster. In its first major action only one out of 28 legionnaires survived, but this formed the basis of the legend of men who would rather die with dignity than surrender.

Legionnaires have fought in the Crimea, in the Franco-Prussian War and against the Paris Commune in 1871. They fought the bare-breasted Amazons of the King of Dahomey in 1892, while 5,736 men died of fever and seven were killed in the action to sub-due Madagascar. They lost 10,000 officers and men, a quarter of their total dead, in Indo-China.

The Legionnaires' motto is 'Legio Patria Nostra' ('The Legion is our Country'). They march at 88 steps a minute, and their patron saint is St Michael.

Every Camerone Day the wooden hand of Captain Danjou, a Legionnaire who died with most of his 63 men in 1863 when faced by 2,000 Mexicans near the village of Camerone in Mexico, is removed from its glass case at the Legion induction centre at Aubagne near Marseilles, paraded on a bed of silk and saluted by bands, cannon-fire and marching men.

Now down to 8,000 men, the Legion has units in Corsica, Djibouti, the Indian Ocean island of Mayotte, Devil's Island, the Pacific nuclear test site at Moruroa Atoll and, most recently, in the Gulf.

One unit, the crack Second Parachute Regiment, the Deuxième REP, has men of 45 nationalities serving in it. Only one in six of the 8,000 volunteers who offer their services each year are accepted.

After three weeks' training at the induction centre, the Legionnaires are automatically committed to a five-year contract. Their names are changed, and they earn the *droit d'asile*, the right to asylum under French law. Officially they cease to exist. In one case, this prevented an Austro-Hungarian aristocrat from learning that he had inherited a 12-million-crown fortune.

Less well known is La Legion Española, whose battle-cry is 'Viva la muerte' ('Long live death'). Recruited almost exclusively from native-born Spaniards, its 7,000 troops are currently garrisoned on the Canary Islands and in the Spanish enclaves of Ceuta and Melilla on the Moroccan coast.

Inspired by the French Foreign Legion, the Spanish force was founded by Colonel José Millan Astray. When he led his newly-formed Legion into action, he was shot in the chest and leg, lost most of his arm and an eye, but survived.

It was in the Legion that Francisco Franco, the future dictator of Spain, first rose to prominence as the youngest general, not only in the Spanish army but also in Europe.

The Legion today survives in a much-reduced form. They still sing their hymn *The Fiancé of Death*, still tattoo themselves with death's heads, and still venerate the memory, and the carefully-preserved eye, of their founder.

Baikalskoye

Brown Bear Coast

IRKUTSK

Olkhon
Island

Sarma

Irkutsk

Lake Baikal in Siberia holds one-fifth of the planet's fresh water and is the deepest lake in the world, measuring more than a mile (1,637 metres) in depth. It was produced by a monumental series of earthquakes, and may mark the start of a new ocean that will divide the north and south parts of Asia.

Possibly created as much as 30 million years ago, this vast and ancient lake contains 5,500 cubic miles of water, almost enough to fill the basins of all five North American Great Lakes. Four hundred miles (645 kms) in surface length, Baikal contains 27 islands and is fed by 336 tributaries but has only one outlet, the Angara river.

In 1990, a joint US-Russian expedition discovered a deep-water hot vent in Baikal, similar to those found on the mid-ocean ridges.

Baikal contains many fishy oddities. The omul is claimed to give a piercing cry when dragged from the icy waters, giving rise to the Russian phrase, 'He cries like an omul', to describe a whiner. Baikal is also the only home of two species of the *golomyanka* fish, the female of which gives birth to 2,000 live young in the autumn. These transparent and buoyant fish, 35 per cent of whose body weight consists of oil, provide food for the lake's indigenous population of nerpa seal, the world's only freshwater seal.

162

In all, Lake Baikal is home to more than 1,550 species of animals and 1,085 species of plants, of which around a thousand are found nowhere else.

Galina Mazepova has spent 24 years studying a tiny species of crayfish that looks like a piece of gravel and lives permanently in its shell on the bottom of the lake. Her thesis on the creature is 477 pages long.

QUELEA

There are more red-billed quelea *(Quelea quelea)* in the world than any other species of bird – several billion, in fact. They form huge colonies, breeding in tropical Africa and migrating south in such huge numbers that they have been compared to swarms of locusts.

Humans have been battling to save their crops from the queleas since the dawn of agriculture, as inscriptions on ancient tombs testify. All manner of whips, rattles, drums and other bird-scaring devices have traditionally been employed, to be joined in modern times by such weapons as mortar bombs, flame-throwers, explosives, poison gas and aerial spraying. Effective methods of control have still not been found.

GIFT-GIVING

According to a business gift-giving guide compiled in 1982 for the Parker Pen Company by Kathleen Reardon, a communication sciences professor at the University of Connecticut, one should avoid black, purple and the number 13 in Latin America; in China one should not give a clock, since it is the same word as funeral in Chinese; in Japan one should not offer a gift depicting a fox or a badger – the fox stands for fertility, the badger for cunning. 'Fifteen-petal chrysanthemums are acceptable, but the 16-petal chrysanthemum is used in the Imperial Family crest and should not be used commercially.'

DIAMONDS

Diamonds are an unstable form of carbon that is continuously reverting to graphite. This is happening so slowly that, at normal room temperature, a diamond will survive for longer than the present age of the Universe.

Synthetic diamonds, first made by the General Electric Co. in 1955, are produced by mixing graphite with either of the metal solvents cobalt or nickel, and subjecting it to temperatures of 2,420°F (1,327°C) and pressures of 60,000 atmospheres. Some 100 million carats of synthetic diamonds are produced annually worldwide.

The combination of great strength, chemical inertness and transparency to infra-red light led to diamond windows being used on the NASA space probe to Venus in 1978. It was the only material that could withstand the cold and vacuum of space, Venus's atmospheric temperature of 920°F (493°C) and pressures a hundred times that of Earth. Diamonds are excellent conductors of heat. Most are brown and yellow and are fit only for industrial use – the colours being produced by atomic-sized imperfections and impurities.

In his book *The Diamond Invention*, Edward Jay Epstein claims that the romantic associations attached to the stone have been artificially created and maintained by the South African based De Beers cartel, which was founded by Cecil Rhodes. 'Diamonds are forever', the official slogan of the company, is another myth. Epstein writes: 'Even though diamonds can be shattered, chipped, discoloured or incinerated to ash, the concept of eternity perfectly captured the magical qualities that they wished to attribute to diamonds.'

It is conservatively estimated that the total weight of cut diamonds that exist in the world is some 500 million carats. A carat is an ancient unit of measurement based on the weight of a carob seed, now set at $^1/_{142}$ ounce (0.2 gms).

If the value of the market is to be maintained, these must be prevented from reaching the market, so the public must be psychologically inhibited from ever parting with their diamonds.

De Beers controls the mining, distribution, cutting, polishing and selling of 80 per cent of all diamonds. In their unmarked fortress off Holborn Circus they control virtually the entire world supply of uncut diamonds. De Beers is part of the Anglo-American and Consolidated Goldfields groups, which were controlled from 1957 to 1984 by Harry Oppenheimer. No other commodity has been so tightly controlled by one man.

The largest uncut diamond ever found was discovered on 25 January 1905, by Captain M.E. Wells in the Premier mine at Cullinan, near Pretoria, South Africa. The Cullinan Diamond, presented to Edward VII by the South African Government, weighed 3,106 carats in its uncut form. The task of transforming it into a finished gem was given to Isaac Asscher, who had to 'cut' the diamond using only a hammer and a fine chisel. (Nowadays cutters use computers to analyse the stones and high-speed diamond saws to cut them.)

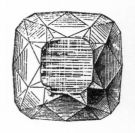

He studied the stone for nine months, knowing that one false blow could break the greatest diamond in the world into pieces. Finally, he steeled himself and made the first strike, confirmed he'd got it right – and then fainted away. His work produced the largest cut diamond in the world, the Star of Africa (530 carats), which forms part of the British Royal Sceptre.

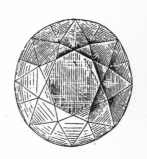

The second largest – the Lesser Star of Africa – is also in the Crown Jewels. The third largest is the De Beers' 'Centenary Diamond', weighing 273 carats, which was unveiled on 1 May 1991 at the Tower of London. Insured for £58 million ($82m), it took three years to cut it from a 599-carat rough stone also discovered at Cullinan on 17 July 1986.

The world's largest heart-shaped diamond is a flawless 70.03-carat gem called 'Le Grand Coeur d'Afrique', which forms the centrepiece of a 50-diamond necklace of heart-shaped stones. It was cut from a 278-carat rough diamond found in the Kankan region of Guinea, West Africa. The operation in New York took nine months. It was sold in 1984 for an undisclosed sum, reputed to be around £5 million ($7m), to one of two billionaires who were bidding against each other for this unique stone.

Diamonds are found in huge numbers in meteorites, a discovery first made in 1970. These tiny diamonds, each containing only a few thousand atoms, are very common but the mystery remained as to how they were formed. The answer is in supernova explosions, according to evidence presented to the American Astronomical Society in 1992 by Donald Clayton of Clanson University in North Carolina.

EGGS

Alain Chatillon keeps a million snails at his escargot stud in Renre-le-Château, south-west France. Each produces one-tenth of an ounce (2.8 gms) of eggs a year, and these are sold as a gourmet delicacy in top restaurants at a cost equivalent to £1,000 ($1,420) per pound (453 gms). He claims to have first discovered snails' eggs during a trip to Tibet in 1979.

The traditional Chinese '1,000-year-old-egg' or 'pei-tan' is actually only a month or so old. It can cause brain damage and attack the central nervous system, according to a 1983 report by Hong Kong's Consumer Council. Traditionally eaten at banquets to usher in the Chinese New Year, the eggs have been revealed to contain five times the legal limit of lead, which comes from the mud-like coating in which they are preserved.

A chicken's egg shell is made of calcium carbonate and has hundreds of tiny pores that allow moisture to evaporate and oxygen to replace it, thus maintaining a perfect internal environment.

In the 21 days an egg takes to incubate, it will absorb more than 8 pints (4.5 litres) of oxygen and release about 7 pints (3.9 litres) of carbon dioxide and $17^1/_2$ pints (9.9 litres) of water vapour.

The largest egg laid by any bird in proportion to its size is that of the brown kiwi (Apteryx australis). The record is of a $3^1/_2$-lb (1.7-kg) hen laying an egg weighing 14 ounces (396 gms). To put it another way, the chicken-sized kiwi lays an egg ten times as large as a hen's. Kiwis have been found dead in their burrows with fully developed eggs inside them.

The smallest egg in relation to body size is that of the emperor penguin (Aptenodytes forsteri), which weighs 1.4 per cent of its body weight.

The largest bird's egg ever laid was that of the now extinct elephant bird (Aepyornis maximus), the smallest that of the vervain hummingbird. One egg of the former, which was a foot (30 cms) long, could contain 33,000 eggs of the latter, and had a shell 75 times as thick.

Each of the seven species of flightless elephant bird was an estimated 10 foot (3 metres) high, weighed 1,000 lbs (450 kgs) and was mainly vegetarian – the biggest and strangest birds ever to walk the Earth. They spawned many myths and legends. Marco Polo claimed they were 'gryphon birds' which could carry an elephant. In the *Arabian Nights,* Sinbad was carried away by the 'rukh' or 'roc'. The birds inspired H.G. Wells to write a story called 'Aepyornis Island', in which a giant egg hatches out to produce a chick that grows 15 feet (4.5 metres) high.

When the first intact *Aepyornis* egg reached Paris in 1850 it caused a sensation. By 1957, there were a reported 29 such eggs in European museums.

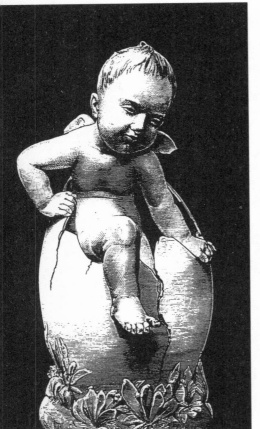

In March 1991, the *New England Journal of Medicine* reported the case of an unnamed 88-year-old man whose compulsive behaviour had led him to eat 24 soft-boiled eggs every day for at least 30 years. A medical investigation discovered that, far from having an increased risk of heart disease, the man had remarkably low blood cholesterol levels. This was due to the fact that he had unusually efficient biological mechanisms that allowed only a tiny amount of the cholesterol from the eggs to be absorbed into his bloodstream.

Between six and eight per cent of all eggs laid are damaged or broken before they reach the consumer; worldwide this damage costs the producers more than $600 million annually.

The largest egg collection in the world is at the Zoological Museum at Tring, Hertfordshire, part of the British Museum (Natural History) and contains an estimated one million eggs. It contains many rarities, including the egg of the extinct Syrian ostrich *(Struthio camelus syriacus),* which was once owned by Colonel T.E. Lawrence (of Arabia).

Classifying and cataloguing the collection has proved to be an immense and difficult task, made more so by the fact that, between 1975 and 1979, a frequent visitor to the museum systematically stole an estimated 30,000 eggs, of which only one-third were recovered, before being apprehended and subsequently convicted. The thief often substituted specimens from elsewhere in the collection to replace the stolen eggs and, in some instances, deleted and replaced registration numbers to conceal his activities.

How can you tell whether an egg is liquid or solid inside? According to Professor Silvanus P. Thompson, writing in the *Journal of the Institution of Electrical Engineers* in 1915, this is how you do it.

'Place an egg on a smooth table, and, holding it between the hands, give it a spin on its side. Then stop it for a moment by laying one finger on it. Then lift the finger off. If it is a solid egg, hard boiled, it remains stationary. If it is a liquid egg, the moment one takes one's finger off, the egg begins to rotate again because the liquid has not ceased running round inside.'

Peter Carl Fabergé (1846–1920), the Russian jeweller, created 54 jewelled Easter eggs for the Tsar and European royalty, of which 47 are known to survive. In 1985 one fetched $1.76 million at auction, being bought by the late billionaire Malcolm Forbes, taking his collection to 11, one more than the Kremlin.

The last Fabergé egg to be auctioned was 'The Love Trophy Egg', commissioned by Tsar Nicholas II to celebrate the birth of his son Alexei at Easter 1905. Bidding opened at $3 million.

Annual US egg consumption has plummeted from 309 per person in 1970 to 234 in 1990, largely because of fears of cholesterol.

An 82-year-old US judge was forcibly retired in 1977 after he kept falling asleep on duty, earning himself the nickname 'Dozy' in legal circles. He once wore a Shirley Temple wig in chambers and refused to take it off when he went into court.

The expression 'kangaroo court' is an Americanism for the illegal trial of an Australian gold digger. It was coined to describe the rough legal justice meted out to Australians who joined the California gold rush in 1849, by vigilante committees set up to try to control their wild behaviour.

The longest Act of Parliament is the parchment of the British Land Tax Act of 1791; it is 1,170 feet (356 metres) long, and was entirely handwritten.

What might well be the longest running court case in history, which began in ancient Egypt around 1350 BC, was finally resolved in 1978, with the rediscovery of the verdict.

The case concerned a squabble over 50 acres (20 hectares) of prime Nile Valley land between various branches of the family of a shipmaster named Neshi. Archaeologists discovered details of the entire case on the walls of the private tomb of one of the plaintiffs, a civil servant called Mose. The only detail missing was the verdict – and the tomb fragments were scattered between Cairo, Sydney and Hanover.

Gabbala Ali Gaballa, an Egyptian scholar, finally tracked it down and discovered that Mose had been triumphant.

Two-thirds of the world's lawyers live in the US – 55,000 of them in Washington, DC alone – a country rightly famed for the quantity and absurdity of its lawsuits. For instance, a man tried to commit suicide by jumping in front of a train and then successfully sued the New York City Transit Authority for $650,000 for the injury he suffered in his failed attempt on his own life.

In another case, a contestant in the 'World's Strongest Man' contest was awarded more than $1 million damages after hurting his knee while running a 40-yard (36-metre) dash with a fridge strapped to his back.

In 1984 the Tasmanian Supreme Court awarded £1,900 ($2,700) in damages to a man who still vomits at the sight of bread, four years after finding a dead mouse in a loaf.

In Vancouver, British Columbia, a man was acquitted on charges of starting a forest fire, despite testimony from a police officer that the man had, while in custody, fallen on his knees, raised his hands and said, 'Oh God, please let me get away with it, just this once.'

On 10 September 1980, the British Columbia Appeal Court rejected the arguments for the defence that this prayer was a privileged communication meant to be heard by God. They ordered a retrial, claiming that God is not a person and what you say to God is admissible as evidence in court.

A judge at Cardiff Crown Court on 19 May 1989 had to halt a fraud trial after the defendant handed him a note saying that her lips were sealed with superglue 'to draw attention to the mistrial and injustice in this court'.

A defence lawyer in Sonora, California, appealed against the sentence of a client convicted of breaking and entering, because the prosecuting attorney 'farted about 100 times' during his closing speech to the jury.

CHINCHILLAS

Chinchillas are small Andean rodents whose hair was used by the Incas to weave a very soft cloth and whose skin was used to line mantles and cloaks. The Spaniards sent large numbers of furs to the courts of Europe and the hunting continued until, in the 1920s, the chinchilla was considered commercially extinct.

After the First World War, an American mining engineer named Chapman conceived the idea of chinchilla fur farms. He obtained permission from the Chilean Government to take some breeding stock to the US, but it took him five years to get  four males and seven females. (Sources vary on the details. *Facts About Furs* claims it took him three years to get 15 specimens.)

The journey from the Andes to the coast took a further three years in order to acclimatize the animals gradually to the changes in altitude and temperature. It took Chapman another 40 days to reach California, with the chinchillas packed in ice as they crossed the Equator. They arrived in Los Angeles in mid-winter, at a time that coincided with their natural moult, shivering and wrapped in blankets.

Somehow they survived and these few provided the breeding stock for the chinchilla ranches. According to a 1979 issue of *Fur Age Weekly*, there are 200,000 small-scale breeding farms in the US alone, each owning an average of ten chinchillas.

Chinchillas are now raised in captivity in every country in Western Europe, as well as Canada, South Africa, India and Poland.

VANILLA

Vanilla is derived from an orchid native to Mexico, where it is pollinated by a small stingless bee, the melipona. Discovered by the Spaniards in the sixteenth century, it was used by the Aztecs to flavour the drink they called xoco-latl. The name for the vanilla bean comes from the Spanish *vainilla,* meaning 'a little seed'.

It was grown only in Mexico until a method of hand-pollination was devised in the mid-nineteenth century. Now about 80 per cent of all vanilla is grown in the Malagasy Republic and the neighbouring islands of Reunion and Comores. Small amounts are also grown in Java, Tahiti and India.

In the Malagasy Republic the flowers of the orchid open in the morning and last for one day. During the season (October to December) women go from flower to flower before noon, lifting the tongues of the bloom and pressing the stamens and pistils together. One woman can pollinate 2,500 flowers in a single day.

The long yellow-green pods are picked when unripe, plunged into boiling water and then packed tightly in tins so that they sweat. They turn dark after a time and become covered with a crystalline substance known as vanillin. The scent is produced by enzyme activity.

The Marquis de Frangipani, an Italian perfume maker living in Paris at the time of Louis XIII, used vanilla with bitter almonds for perfuming gloves and handkerchiefs. He devised his own vanilla ice-creams and a thick cream filling for pastry that still bears his name *(frangipani).*

UNDERGROUND

The air in Moscow's subway stations is changed four times every hour.

The world's biggest volume of traffic in an underground railway system is Tokyo's, which carries five million passengers every day.

The US Department of Agriculture's dairy mountain is stored deep underground in man-made caves cut into the hills round Kansas City, Missouri, and in some 500 other locations in more than 30 states.

In November 1982 these stores held 400 million lbs (180m kgs) of butter stored in great frozen blocks at 0°F (-17°C), 1,150 million lbs (520m kgs) of dried milk in 50-lb (23-kg) bags, and 800 million lbs (360m kgs) of cheese.

There are 143,000 miles (230,000 kms) of sewers and 198,000 miles (318,000 kms) of water-mains in the United Kingdom.

Véronique le Guen, who set a new world record by spending 111 days alone in a cavern 260 feet (80 metres) below ground at Valat-Negre in southern France, commited suicide, some time after her return to the surface, in January 1990, by taking an overdose of barbiturates.

Her record was broken in 1989 by Stefania Follini, who spent 131 days alone in a 20-foot by 12-foot (6 x 3.6-metre) Plexiglass module, sealed 30 feet (9 metres) below ground in a cave in New Mexico.

The world's largest genealogical database, which contains more than 70 million names, is buried in six huge vaults beneath 820 feet (250 metres) of solid granite in the Rocky Mountains to the east of Salt Lake City, Utah. It was compiled by Mormon disciples of the

Church of Jesus Christ of Latter-day Saints. The vaults are designed to hold 26 million books on microfiche, and have their own radiation-proof water supply.

More than 10,000 earth-sheltered homes have been built in North America. In Oklahoma there are 27 subterranean schools. There are underground churches, libraries and factories, and a motel in Jackson, Minnesota called the Earth Inn.

In China, some five million people live more or less underground in either earth houses or converted nuclear shelters.

Underground Vaults and Storage of Hutchinson, Kansas, lease worked-out chambers in a salt mine as archive storage space to corporations, governments and private individuals. Ten acres (4 hectares) of underground chambers – 50 million cubic feet (1,415,000 cu metres) of space – were filled between 1959 and 1983. MGM stores all its colour masters here, including *Gone With The Wind.* Conditions are perfect – a dry, clean atmosphere at constant temperature and pressure.

Biologists at Bangor University College in Wales created a rhizotron – an 'underground observatory' – in 1988 for studying how soil creatures interact with plant life. Essentially it was a bunker sunk into a field, its sides filled with glass viewing panels, microscopic lenses and cameras. Dr Charmain Sackville Hamilton reported, 'We spend a lot of time watching the worms go by.'

The Civil and Mineral Engineering Building at the University of Minnesota is an 'earthscraper' ten storeys deep, a $16.7 million complex of labs, offices and lecture rooms. Natural light is 'piped' through the building using a series of lenses and mirrors – a whole new technology based on the delivery of light, rather than the delivery of electricity to be transformed into light. The building also houses what is believed to be the world's biggest periscope, 132 feet (40 metres) high; this enables a three-dimensional image of the outside world to be seen on a 2-foot by 3-foot (0.6 x 0.9-metre) window on the seventh level – a room with a view, 110 feet (34 metres) below ground.

While making an inventory of the 600–700 tunnels and caves beneath the streets of Nottingham in 1988 researchers discovered a huge Victorian rock carving of Daniel in the Lion's Den.

Beneath the streets of London lie 100 miles (161 kms) of neolithic rivers, 1,500 miles (2,400 kms) of neo-Gothic sewers, 82 miles (132 kms) of tube tunnels and 16 miles (26 kms) of British Telecom tunnels.

VEGETABLES

The world's first and only potato museum was founded at the International School in Brussels and was last heard of in Washington, DC. It contains potato music written by Johann Sebastian Bach, potato jewellery, potato puppets, potato quilts, paper made from potatoes and pots made from potato peelings (potato mâché?). It informs visitors that there are more than 5,000 varieties of potatoes, and that Marie Antoinette wore potato flowers in her hat to popularize the plant.

Lettuce has been eaten by humans since at least 800 BC. Lettuce seeds have been found in Egyptian tombs. Cos lettuce got its name from its place of origin, the Greek island of Cos.

The Department of Vegetable Crops at the University of California at Davis spent 25 years trying to develop a square or oblong tomato. They succeeded in 1977 with a square tomato, codenamed UC-82, designed to better survive mechanical harvesting.

According to Greek legend, cabbages originally sprang from Zeus' sweat.

In March 1990, the Arabic characters for Allah were reportedly found inside aubergines in Nottingham and Leicester by devout Muslims. Some 5,000 pilgrims travelled from all over the Midlands to see these curious vegetables.

In July 1989, a 56-year-old man was killed after being struck in the back by a turnip thrown from a moving car. At the inquest his death was linked with 23 other incidents throughout London's East End in which melons, potatoes and cabbages had been thrown in the same manner. The police said they were treating the case as murder.

The 'spinach myth' celebrated in the Popeye cartoons – according to which spinach is a rich source of iron, and thus of strength – has been debunked by the British Nutrition Foundation.

The myth appears to have originated in 1870 when a certain Dr E. Von Wolf wrongly analysed the vegetable's iron content. His figure passed into medical literature and remained unchecked for 50 years.

In 1937 a certain Professor Schuphan reanalysed these findings and discovered the iron content in spinach was one-tenth that claimed by Von Wolf, and was much the same as in any similar dark green leafy vegetable.

TAXONOMY

The science of classifying animals and plants contains many curiosities, including a salamander named *Oedipus complex*; a fish named *Boops Boops*; the greater hoopoe *Upupa epops*; a genus of clams *Abra,* with a species called *Abra cadabera*; hard-skinned fossil fish with the names of *Ptomaspis, Dikenaspis* and *Ariaspis* (Tom, Dick and Harry); sea urchins called *Disaster*; a species of wasp called *Aha ha*; snails called *Trivia* and *Anticlimax*; an indecently exposed fungus called *Phallus impudicus*; a fossil dinosaur named *Scrotum humanum*; and an alga named *Hummbrella* in honour of Dr Humm.

In 1904 the entomologist G.W. Kirkaldy created the bug genera *Pollychisme* (Polly-kiss-me), *Peggichisme, Marichisme, Dolichisme* and *Florichisme*.

A nineteenth-century taxonomist named Leach named a host of parasitic isopods after his wife Caroline, each genus carrying an anagram of her name: *Lironeca, Nerocila, Rocinela,* etc.

In 1926 Dybowski named a species of tiny crustacean *Cancelloidokytodermogammarus (Loveninus-kytodermogammarus) loveni*, honouring it with the longest name in the organic world.

One taxonomist, who lost patience while trying to make sense of a very complex group of ants, ended up naming *Stenamma exasperata*.

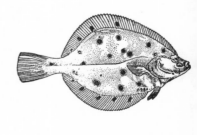

AA HARTWEGII

Aa Hartwegii is the Latin name of a rare species of orchid found only in the high Andes of Venezuela, where it grows near the extreme limit of plant life at an altitude of around 13,000 feet (4,000 metres).

This unusual alphabetical concoction was revealed to me in a 1983 letter from G.C.K. Dunsterville in Venezuela, who sent a copy of his article on the subject which appeared in the *American Orchid Society Bulletin* (Volume 52, Number 1, January 1983), along with a collection of other taxonomic oddities. He writes: 'Various reasons have been put forward to explain why the famous orchid taxonomist H.G. Reichenbach invented and published this very odd name of *Aa* in 1854, but the one that appeals to me most is that he did it to ensure that a Reichenbach genus would for all eternity stand at the head of any alphabetical list of genera – not only of orchids or even of plants, but of anything that was living, had lived or some day might live on the face of this globe or outside it. Which is quite an achievement to attain by the mere publication of a two-lettered name for a taxonomic group!'

Galfrid Clement Keyworth Dunsterville was born on 18 February 1905, and died on 26 November 1988. He inherited the nickname 'Stalky' from his father, who had been the original for Kipling's hero in *Stalky & Co.*

After a 34-year career in the oil industry with Shell, he devoted his retirement to the study and illustration of orchids. His *Venezuelan Orchids Illustrated* (6 vols), co-authored with Dr Leslie Garay, is the definitive work and took 18 years to complete. The almost limitless variety of orchids is indicated by the fact that on one trip to the Andes, on one tree alone, he counted 48 different species.

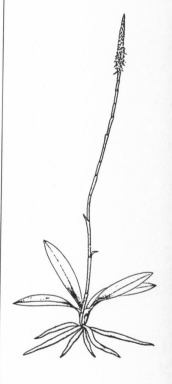

In September 1983, at Barnham Broom course, a ball driven by golfer Les King, of Wymondham, Norfolk, landed in a river and stunned a 2-foot (60-cm) pike.

According to Phillips, the London auction house, between 1988 and 1990 old golf balls outperformed all other investments. The record auction price is £8,500 ($12,000), paid by a Connecticut collector for a mid-nineteenth-century ball stitched together and stuffed with boiled goose feathers. When just made, these 'feathery balls' cost between two and five shillings, the equivalent of £80–120 ($110–170) now. Golf was thus a rich man's game until the rubber-bound core ball was invented in the early years of this century.

Thomas J. Caradonio, a 70-year-old golf enthusiast, was buried in Houston in August 1984 wearing full golfing regalia and holding a golf putter in his right hand.

The most remote golf course in the United Kingdom is on its own island – Grunay – in the Outer Skerries off the Shetlands. The nine-hole course, set in 58 acres, was offered for sale in 1984 at £45,000 ($64,000). The price included two houses, an outboard dinghy and sheep that act as greenkeepers.

In 1986 the US Senior Professional Golf Association (PGA) tour was dominated by one of the most unlikely champions in its history – a 56-year-old half-blind black man, with a crippled and contorted body, named Charlie Owens. A former college football star for the Chicago Bears, Owens damaged one leg after parachuting on to a tree stump in Korea. Years on the pro circuit led to problems with his other knee, his ankle and back. His throat was scarred from a stabbing, one of many incidents in a crowded domestic life involving four wives and five children. His turn of fortune came with 'a vision from God' of an armpit-high putter that accommodates his arthritis and bursitis.

The huge numbers of golfers in Japan and the exorbitant cost of new golf balls (more than £22/$30 for a six-pack) has made the recycling of lost balls a £17 million ($24m)-a-year business. They resell at one-third of the cost of new balls.

'Ducks' are the trade name for professional collectors who specialize in retrieving balls from golf-course ponds. Some can earn up to £25,000 ($35,500) a year at their clandestine task; one was found dead in 1988 at the bottom of a pond after his breathing apparatus failed. The Supreme Court ruled in April 1988 that stray balls belong to the golf course. One prestige course drained its pond and found 50,000 lost balls.

There are more than 13 million golfers in Japan, but only around 1,200 golf courses. Foursomes are forced to tee off at four-minute intervals, so there is little time to search for lost balls.

China's biggest golf club, the 18-hole Peking International, is financed by Japanese corporations and is designed to cater for Japanese businessmen. Membership fees (£12,000/$17,000) are equal to a peasant's earnings for 177 years.

The Elephant Hills Country Club golf course in Zimbabwe includes such hazards as sleeping buffalo and roaming warthogs. One local rule states that if a baboon picks up a ball, the player can hit another but only if he retrieves the original within three minutes.

Angelo Spagnola is the only known person officially

to hold a US PGA title as the worst golfer. He won this distinction after an 18-hole round of 257 on the Ponte Verde course in Florida. He took 66 strokes to get from one hole to the next.

Where did golf originate? The most widely accepted view is Scotland, the first recorded reference being a 1457 statute which decreed that the 'unproffitable' sports of football and golf should be 'utterly cryed downe' because they were interfering with archery practice.

However there have been many rival claims, the most surprising of which was published in a 1991 issue of the *Australian Society for Sports History Bulletin*. Professor Ling Hong-Ling claims that a game called Chiuwan (*chiu* means 'hitting', *wan* means 'ball') was first documented in Chinese literature in AD 943 and remained popular until the eighteenth century. He suggests traders took the game to Europe in the Middle Ages, where it was developed and refined into golf. Evidence for this claim is found in illustrations on pottery and in murals.

TIME CAPSULES

At the 1939 New York World's Fair, a 'time capsule' (a term coined by the event's publicist), made of copper alloy and designed to be opened in AD 6,939 was buried. It contained ten million words of microfilmed essays, reproductions of works by Picasso, a Bible, the Lord's Prayer in 300 languages, a rhinestone clip from Woolworths, baseball cards, a toothbrush and a copy of *Weird Tales*. There were also messages to the future from luminaries like Einstein and Thomas Mann, contained in a book, printed on special paper in non-fading ink, that was also sent to libraries and monasteries throughout the world.

The contents of the Westinghouse time capsule buried in 1964 at the World's Fair in Flushing, Queens, New York, next to the original, included: twenty million words of microfilmed text, the Bible, a piece of heat shield from a spacecraft, a *National Geographic* World Atlas (in microfilm), freeze-dried food, a bikini, *A Hard Day's Night* by the Beatles, a plastic heart valve, an electronic watch, a pocket radiation-detector, a phial of desalted Pacific Ocean water, a ruby laser rod, a bottle of tranquillizers, a bottle of antibiotics, a ballpoint pen, a rechargeable flashlight, graphite from the first nuclear reactor, a container of Carbon 14, a tektite mineral of possible lunar origin, film history of the USS *Nautilus*, credit cards, a transistor radio, 20 Kent filter cigarettes, a Polaroid camera, an electric toothbrush, zirconium metal, a computer memory unit, contact lenses, a ceramic magnet, a molecular block, birth-control pills, *Echo II* satellite material, a satellite radio receiver, a piece of re-entry shield from Scott Carpenter's *Aurora 7* spacecraft, a dish of pyroceram, sequoia wood, synthetic fibres, a roll of superconducting wire, fuel cells, irradiated seeds, a fibre-reinforced metal, a radiation-detecting film badge, a roll of film of Calder Hall (the world's first nuclear power station) and a plastic wrapper. The capsule is to be opened on the same day as the first.

According to the International Time Capsule Society, many capsules have now been lost because nobody can remember where they were buried.

A time capsule containing the signatures of 22 million Americans, which was to have been interred by President Ford to immortalize the US Bicentennial on 4 July 1976, was stolen from an unattended van.

ZUNI

This tribe of native Americans call themselves 'The Children of the Sun' and they have an interesting creation myth, as told in *Pueblo Gods and Myths* by H.A. Tyler.

'In the beginning of the new-made, the All-container conceived within himself and thought outward in space, whereby mists of increase, steams potent of growth, were evolved and uplifted . . . he made himself in person and form of the Sun whom we hold to be our father . . . and with the brightening of the spaces the great mist-clouds were thickened together and fell . . . impregnating the world-holding sea.'

HANGOVERS

The Finnish slang dictionary has 29 entries for hangover (plus 102 expressions for being drunk). These include: *lasirokko* ('glasspox') and *pienat sepat* ('little smiths' – i.e. pounding in the brain).

The people of Chicago say of a hangover, 'It was very drunken out last night . . . '

From Spain and Portugal comes *resaca*, which is the pounding of breakers on a rocky promontory, while the best from Burma is *gaungit*, which evokes 'that which, while it lasts, makes a man feel that the clapper of the heaviest temple bell for miles around is playing tunes on the inside of his skull'.

Buster Keaton's favourite hangover cure was one raw egg in a glass of cold beer with tomato ketchup added.

QUEEN'S MESSENGERS

Britain's 40 Queen's Messengers are a select corps of trusted couriers headed by Superintendent Lieutenant-Colonel Ernest Crump. In 1977 they carried 342 tonnes of correspondence, covering a distance of 7 million miles (11m kms) at a cost to the taxpayer of £1.9 million ($2.7m). They carry diplomatic bags to overseas embassies, containing messages and objects too sensitive to travel unaccompanied, such as secret intelligence reports and parts for decoding machines. Under the terms of the 1961 Vienna Convention on Diplomatic Relations, they may not be searched or detained.

The emblem of the corps is a silver leaping greyhound, which has been in use since the time of Charles II.

OVEREATERS VICTORIOUS

Overeaters Victorious Inc. is a group from Minneapolis that believes in 'dieting with Jesus'. Suggested reading for the group includes *God's Answer to Fat* by Frances Hunter and *More of Jesus, Less of Me* by Joan Cavanaugh.

Ms Cavanaugh recommends that Christian dieters should 'only buy foods that Jesus, John or Peter would buy'. She continues: 'God gives us the good stuff. I can't imagine Jesus Christ coming out of the supermarket with twelve bags of chips, one for each apostle.'

METEORITES

The largest known meteorite, a 60-tonne lump of iron and nickel, was found in 1920 at Hoba Farm near Grootfontein in Namibia.

One of the largest meteorite falls in recorded history consisted of the four tonnes of fragments that fell in the Jilin province of north-east China on 8 March 1976. The largest lump weighed about two tonnes, and made a hole $6\frac{1}{2}$ feet (2 metres) wide and 21 feet (6.5 metres) deep when it hit the ground. Scientists estimate that the meteorite from which the fragments came was a lump of rock about 5 feet (1.5 metres) across, which had been travelling through interplanetary space for about 400,000 years.

Nelson Morgan Davis, an eccentric Canadian businessman who died in March 1979, bought a meteorite that landed near Cleveland for $10,000, had it crushed and transported to his Toronto home, where he used it to cover his driveway with its chemically-inert and dust-free gravel, in order to stop visitors tracking dirt into his living room.

It is likely that more actuaries live and work in the area around Hartford, Connecticut, where the giant US insurance business is centred, than anywhere else in the world. (Actuaries calculate the statistical risks and premiums for all kinds of accidents, injuries and disasters on behalf of the insurance industry.)

Wethersfield is a small Connecticut town of 26,000 people, and it has been struck by meteorites twice in 11 years.

In April 1971 a $12\frac{1}{2}$-ounce (0.3-kg) meteorite struck a house, crashing through the roof and becoming embedded in the ceiling of the living room. Then on 8 November 1982, a 6-lb (2.7-kg) meteorite tore into another house while its owners were watching *M*A*S*H* on television. Travelling at 300 mph (483 km/h), it burst through the roof, an upstairs closet, and the living-room ceiling, hit the floor, bounced off at an angle into the dining room, ricocheted off the ceiling and finally rolled under the dining-room table.

The odds against two meteorites striking houses in the same town is incalculable. In the whole of recorded history, fewer than a dozen houses are known to have been struck. Only one city, Honolulu, is known to have been struck twice by meteorites (in 1825 and 1949) but no houses were hit on either occasion.

On 7 April 1990, a meteorite 10 inches (25 cms) across hit a house in the Dutch town of Enschede, shattering roofing tiles, penetrating 4 inches (10 cms) of insulating material, and breaking into fragments in an upstairs bedroom.

A much bigger meteorite exploded 6.2 miles (10 kms) above the northern Dutch province of Friesland in August 1992.

The first recorded meteorite to hit Britain for 26 years fell in the back garden of a house in the village of Glatton, near Peterborough, in May 1991.

Since the 1970s more than 10,000 meteorites have been found in Antarctica; 11 of them turned out to be pieces of the moon.

The whole course of geological and biological evolution on Earth may have been altered several times by the impact of meteorites or comets striking the Earth. The mass extinction of more than half of all living species, including the last of the dinosaurs, at the end of the Cretaceous period, 65 million years ago, may have been caused by just such an impact;

the explosion would have been equivalent to a million eruptions of Mount St Helens.

The principal evidence for this has been provided by the discovery of more than 120 known meteoric impact craters around the world, the first of which was identified by Daniel M. Barringer in 1905 near Flagstaff, Arizona. Now known as Meteor Crater, it is 4,000 feet (1,200 metres) in diameter and 400 feet

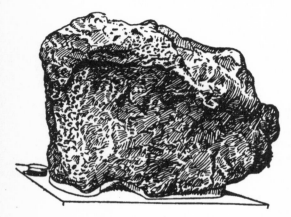

(120 metres) deep. It was formed by an iron meteorite, an estimated 200 feet (60 metres) in diameter and weighing approximately one million tonnes. It probably hit the Earth at a speed of about 9 miles (15 kms) per second, creating an explosion equivalent to 20 million tonnes of TNT.

Seventy per cent of all meteorites land in the ocean, but the only underwater impact crater discovered to date lies beneath shallow waters off the coast of Nova Scotia. Named the Montagnais Structure, it is 50 million years old and 37 miles (60 kms) wide, and was found in 1987.

The Sudbury Complex in Canada, an elliptical-shaped ring 37 miles (60 kms) long and 17 miles (27 kms) wide, supplies more than one-fifth of the world's nickel, as well as being rich in copper, cobalt, platinum and many other rare minerals. It is believed to be an astrobleme – a mineral deposit formed by the impact of a meteorite 1,840 million years ago.

Only one person is known to have been hit by a meteorite. On 30 November 1954, Mrs Hewlett Hodges of Sylacauga, Alabama, was eating lunch when a 9-lb (4-kg) meteorite crashed through her roof and hit her in the upper thigh. She was not seriously hurt.

On the night of Hallowe'en 1938, Orson Welles and
the Mercury Theatre staged one of the great special
effects of broadcasting, terrifying an entire nation
with their adaptation of H.G. Wells's *The War of the
Worlds.*

The site chosen for the invasion was picked by
chance – the writer Howard Koch dropped his pen-
cil on to a map of New Jersey, and it landed
on Grover's Mill, midway between New
York and Philadelphia.

Los Angeles Times staff writer Marlene
Cimons revisited the spot in October 1979 and
spoke to residents who remembered the night
when 1.5 million Americans ran for cover.

One man told Cimons: 'The Martians
landed in the farm right next door to ours.
We seen all the traffic. Pop says: "These
people are crazy." Hundreds of cars went by
and the road wasn't even paved then. Some of
the people were yellin', "The Martians are coming!" He didn't pay no attention to them. He just
went on husking corn – in them days there were no
combines – and sayin', "They all must be drunk." '

The late Hadley Cantril, then associate professor
of psychology at Princeton University, conducted a
study to determine the reason for the mass hysteria.
He concluded that America was nervous about the
developing war.

'Probably never before in the history of broadcasting had so many people in this country been
glued to their sets,' he wrote. 'Stations at all hours
were willing to interrupt prearranged programs for
the latest broadcast. Hence both the technique and
the content of this broadcast tended to fit into the
existing mental context which had resulted from
world events of the previous weeks.'

William Hill of Atlanta had his treasured garbage collection removed from his house in January 1975. He had packed his three-room dwelling with bottles, cans, papers, old fish heads – in fact anything he could find. According to his sister, Mrs Evelyn Murin, who had to move out as a result, he boasted that he was going to make big money with his collection.

In 1982 Ronald Raffill, a 68-year-old bachelor who lived alone in a bungalow in Deerbarn Road, Guildford, was found dead in a five-tonne mountain of rubbish that he had accumulated in his living room.

In 1983 a 49-year-old bank clerk in Paris was found dead in his flat on top of a mountain of garbage that was piled up to within 4 feet (1.2 metres) of the ceiling. Every item had been cleaned before being added to the heap.

Miss Mary Booth, one of two children of a prosperous Bradford wool merchant and eminent naturalist, died in December 1980 aged 76, leaving behind her 1,000 pairs of boxed and unused shoes, 700 bolts and parcels of dress and curtain fabrics and 14 cabin trunks, plus enough costume jewellery to fill five of them, as well as seven large suitcases, two ottomans, some 25,000 books and a tea-chest full of mostly Georgian silver, including 150 vinaigrettes, 32 nutmeg graters, 44 snuff-boxes and 30 punch ladles. In addition there were thousands of newspapers, some dating back to the turn of the century, and hundreds of tins of food. A 1930 Morris Isis Six was found in the garage.

The clearance and sale proved a massive task for the estate agents. A spokesman said: 'There were narrow corridors among the piles of possessions which gave access only to the kitchen sink and through to the hall, where there was just space to squeeze up one edge of the staircase to one of five bedrooms, where it was possible to discern a bed. Otherwise the house was filled in many instances to the height of six feet.'

The house took the auctioneers and a team of students 800 man-hours to clear. Even after the huge auction, and after local charities had their pick, there were still 400 plastic bin-liners, 17 skips and 15 council lorry-loads of valueless items that had to be removed.

NEWTON'S APPLE

The story of the apple falling on Newton's head is one of the classic tales in the history of science. But is it true?

All the accounts of the story seem to date from the last year of Newton's life. Here is the account of John Conduitt, a close associate: 'In the year 1666 he retired again from Cambridge . . . to his mother in Lincolnshire and whilst he was musing in a garden it came into his thought that the power of gravity (which brought an apple from the tree to the ground) was not limited to a certain distance from the earth but that this power must extend much farther than was usually thought.'

Voltaire popularized the story, quoting Catherine Conduitt (John's wife and Newton's niece) as the authority for the apple. Newton's biographer Richard Westfall writes: 'Small wonder that such an anecdote, redolent of the Judaeo-Christian association of the apple with knowledge, continues to be repeated . . . it has contributed to the notion that universal gravitation appeared to Newton in a flash of insight in 1666 and that he carried the *Principia* about with him essentially complete for 20 years until Halley pried it loose and gave it to the world.'

Every circus ring in the world is exactly 42 feet (12.8 metres) in diameter because in 1768 the trick rider Sergeant Major Philip Astley, then serving with a British dragoon regiment, discovered that a circle of that precise size allowed him to stand on a galloping horse because the centrifugal force kept him upright. The following year he staged an equestrian show in London, mixed it with street performers, and the first circus was born.

An old-time Astley's advertisement, showing "The Courier of St. Petersburg", performed by Andrew Ducrow, who invented this act.

The Greatest Show On Earth, the billing Phineas Taylor Barnum gave to his circus, is now a copyrighted name. When John Ringling North took over, one of his greatest stunts was to get Stravinsky to write the music for the elephants' ballet and to hire George Balanchine to choreograph it.

Every clown has a unique 'face', which is his or her 'living'. These are registered with Clowns International by being painted on an eggshell. When a clown dies, his 'face' is buried with him.

The first human cannonball was a woman, Zazel. She was fired 60 feet (18.3 metres) from a cannon on 2 April 1877, at London's Westminster Aquarium. Her act was such a sensation that her original engagement was extended for two years at a salary of £120 ($170) per week. She lived to a ripe old age and died of natural causes in 1937.

Karl Wallenda, one of the foremost wire-walkers in the history of the circus, was the son of a catcher in a flying act. He performed on the wire for 57 years, drawing virtually his entire family into the act and ruling them with an iron hand.

The Great Wallendas had many narrow escapes. They were on the wire when the Hartford fire broke out in the Ringling Brothers circus tent in 1944; 168 people died, but the Wallendas escaped with singed costumes.

To make their act more spectacular, the Wallendas performed without a safety net. Their supreme stunt was the seven-person pyramid, which no act had attempted before or has duplicated since. It fell apart in Detroit, on the night of 30 January 1962; Wallenda's nephew and son-in-law died, and his son Mario was paralysed from the waist down. Karl suffered a fractured pelvis but was back on the wire the following night. A year later his sister-in-law fell 45 feet (14 metres) to her death from a high bar, and in 1972 another son-in-law was electrocuted in front of a live audience in a freak accident.

On 22 March 1978, the 73-year-old Karl fell to his death while attempting to walk 200 feet (60 metres) on a wire strung ten storeys up between two hotels in San Juan, Puerto Rico, in gusty conditions. At his widow's request, the balancing pole he had been carrying on that fatal day was cut into small pieces and auctioned off to raise funds for the Showfolks of Sarasota, a club for members of the circus profession.

The Argentinian Hugo Zamoratte is the circus world's only enterologist. The opposite of escapology, it is the art of getting into confined spaces. When he was nine he had a dream about a king who disappeared into a glass bottle, and told him he would have to learn to do this himself. While doing national service he discovered he could dislocate every joint in his body, painlessly and at will. For a time he worked as an accountant for Fiat by day, and with a freak show at night. Now a fully-fledged professional circus performer, he can squeeze his five-foot nine-inch (1.7-metre) frame into a bottle 18 inches (46 cms) in diameter by systematically dislocating his shoulders, elbows, hips and knees.

OCCUPATIONAL NAMES

Psychologist Lewis Lipsitt of Brown University in Providence, Rhode Island, has spent over ten years collecting examples of people whose names reflect their occupations. He has discovered a birdwatcher names Hawkes, a music teacher called Fiddler, a mailman called Post and a Mr Martini who studies the effects of alcohol on the body.

What began as a piece of frivolous research acquired a deeper significance when Lipsitt discovered that the idea of 'prophetic names' had a long history. Jung reflected on the fact that a man called Herr Gross had feelings of grandeur whilst Herr Klein (German for 'small') had feelings of inferiority. Jung's own name means 'young', and it was he who introduced the idea of rebirth. As Jung wrote, 'Are these the whimsical effects of chance or the suggestions of the name?'

FIRST FLIGHT

Orville and Wilbur Wright may have entered the history books as being the pioneers of manned flight in December 1903, but there are many rival claimants. These include:

• Clément Ader, whose bat-like, steam-driven flying machine may have left the ground in the 1890s at the Château d'Armainvilliers. The French credit Ader as the first aviator.

• Santos-Dumont, a Brazilian who became one of France's foremost balloonists and built an aeroplane out of three box kites and a steam engine, which he flew outside Paris on 23 October 1906. This claim is backed by many aviation historians, who considered that the Wrights achieved only a powered glide.

• Samuel Pierpont Langley, whose catapult-launched plane flew in 1896 – an event witnessed by Alexander Graham Bell.

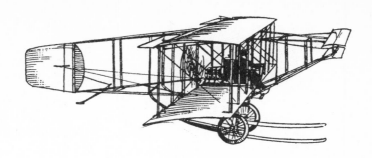

• Lyman Gilmore, a US pioneer aviator, who died penniless in 1951. In 1981 historians discovered a log which claimed that he made a powered flight on 15 May 1902.

• Gustav Whitehead, a German-born engineer, who flew a butterfly-shaped acetylene-powered monoplane on 14 August 1901. This claim is backed by massive documentation and was boosted in December 1987 when a replica of the craft, with a modern engine generating the same power as the original, duplicated Whitehead's claims.

Patrick Alexander, a wealthy British agent and prominent member of the Aeronautical Society of Great Britain, was assigned by the Royal Engineers to watch the development of the Wright Brothers' flying machine.

He befriended them and was actually invited to Kitty Hawk, North Carolina, for the historic 1903 test that resulted in the first powered flight of a motor-driven aeroplane. But Alexander went to the wrong place and missed the event of a lifetime.

An interesting footnote to this story is that news editors all over America ignored the event. Only one paper, *The Norfolk Virginian-Pilot* (the name was pure coincidence), actually headlined it on the front page the following day. Dated 18 December 1903, the headline read: 'FLYING MACHINE SOARS 3 MILES IN TEETH OF HIGH WIND OVER SAND HILLS AND WAVES AT KITTY HAWK ON CAROLINA COAST'.

AUCTIONS

The last lot at the last auction by Harrods, held on 19 November 1981, was the auctioneer's own rostrum, which sold for £14 ($20).

Paul Revere's $190 expense account for his famous 11-day horseback ride from Boston to New York in 1774 was auctioned in April 1978 for more than $10,000.

In June 1980, the biggest private collection of autographs – the life-long obsession of Ray Rawlins, an ex-colonial serviceman and the author of *The Guinness Book of World Autographs* – was auctioned at Sotheby's. His collection of more than 30,000 items included letters or documents signed by every British sovereign since Henry VII, every British Prime Minister and most American Presidents. There was a curt note from Beau Brummel to his tailor, and a letter from General Gordon identifying the island of Praslin in the Seychelles as the site of the Garden of Eden, the coco de mer plant as the Tree of Knowledge, and the bread fruit plant as the Tree of Life.

The auction catalogue identified it as a 'small dried-up object, genteelly described as a mummified tendon taken from Napoleon's body during the post-mortem'. It was put up for auction in London in 1969 by its part-owner, an American named Bruce Gimelson, but the highest price offered for this imperial relic was £17,000 ($24,000), well below the reserve price, and it was withdrawn from sale. A disappointed Mr Gimelson said afterwards, 'You can't put a value on it – it's unique,' and added that he hoped to sell it to the French Government. It was

Napoleon's penis, removed along with several other pieces of his anatomy at a post-mortem.

(The existence of this curio was subsequently denied by a spokesman from the auction house in 1992, who said the story was 'one of the oldest chestnuts in the business'. However, we have the *Daily Mirror* clipping as proof.)

On 10 June 1981, Marilyn Monroe's pink mesh brassière was sold for £520 ($750), in a lot that included a beaded bag and a pair of white evening gloves, to Stanley Marsh III of Toad Hall, Amarillo, Texas, as a present for his wife.

At an auction at Morlaix, France, on 6 June 1979, a collector paid 34,000 francs ($6,000) for Marie Antoinette's bidet.

A pair of Elvis Presley's underpants fetched $605 at a New York auction in June 1988.

An auction in 1981 at Bonham's in London of a collection of bygones and curiosities included the following: a Norman horseshoe, a lamb's pewter feeding bottle, a piece of medieval wooden drainpipe, a scold's bridle, a horse-sweat scraper, an ivory apple corer, a masonic snuff-box and a Georgian tongue-scraper for removing encrustations of port from the palate.

The hospital tag tied to the toe of Lee Harvey Oswald was sold at auction on 11 April 1992 for $6,600. It was bought by gun collector Anthony Pugliese, who had previously purchased for $220,000 the pistol Jack Ruby used to shoot Oswald.

There are 25–30,000 bubblegum-wrapper collectors in the Czech Republic and Slovakia. The largest collection in Britain (18,000 specimens) belongs to Steve Fletcher of north London who, unlike the Czechs, collects both wrappers and contents.

The Kansas Barbed Wire Collectors Association is just one group of an estimated 70,000 'barbarians' in the US who meet annually in La Crosse, Kansas, which bills itself as the 'Barbed Wire Capital of the World'. The first patent for barbed wire was taken out in 1873 by Illinois farmer Joseph Glidden, and his original double-strand design, the Winner, is still the bestseller of all time. He received 25 cents royalty on every hundred-weight of wire sold, enough to make him a millionaire. There are now more than 1,600 different types of barbed wire with names like Split Diamond, Buckthorn, Necktie, Arrow Plate and the Brotherton Barb. The *International Barbed Wire Gazette* is published in Sunset, Texas.

A little-known area of collecting is 'coconut treen' — worked coconut shells which may be elaborately carved or turned into goblets, tumblers, bowls, flasks, caskets or even teapots.

Mervyn Mitton of Bournemouth has the largest and finest collection of police equipment in Britain, including more than 400 truncheons.

The largest collection of bricks in Britain is held by Henry Holt, a retired timber merchant, who has 4,500 different types. The only British member of the International Brick Collectors' Association, he also collects milk bottles.

The world's biggest collection of orange wrappers has been assembled by David and Rosemarie van der Plank of St Ives in Cornwall. They also have the world's biggest collection of matchbox labels.

KAMIKAZE

The Kamikaze Tokubetsu Kogekitai (Kamikaze Special Attack Squad) was formed as a desperate measure to defend Okinawa in April 1945.

It was named after the *Kamikaze* (Divine Wind) sent by the Sun Goddess, which wrecked the huge fleet of the Mogul conqueror Kublai Khan in 1281.

Its suicide pilots were strapped into wooden Okhas which had a 2,640-lb (1,200-kg) bomb built into their fuselage. Released into the air from large bombers, the kamikaze had no parachute, no radio and primitive controls. Few survived the hazardous run-in to the US fleet. Some 7,800 kamikaze died at Okinawa; they cost the US 40 ships sunk, 368 damaged and 763 aircraft.

Haruo Hiroto was the only kamikaze pilot to survive the Second World War. Hiroto was rescued by a US convoy ship when his Okha crash-landed in the ocean. He subsequently became the chef of a French restaurant in Washington, DC.

CONDOMS

Condoms were first used in Rome but not rediscovered until 1,100 years later by the Italian anatomist Gabriel Fallopius, who gave his name to the fallopian tube. His condom consisted of a linen sheath soaked in certain chemicals.

The 'French letter' used to be called the 'French bladder', and consisted of a sheath made of the membrane from the stomach of a young sheep. According to received wisdom, they were imported into England, where they were in great demand for the prevention of venereal disease.

However, a letter in the royal archives at Windsor Castle, discovered in 1987 by the historian Dr Jeremy Black, suggests that the trade operated in reverse, and that *capotes anglaises* (English overcoats) were exported to the court of Louis XIV.

Louis's Master of the Royal Household wrote to Colonel Joseph Yorke, a British diplomat in Paris, asking him 'to procure 300 or more of those preventive machines, made use of by the Gallant tho' prudent young Gentlemen of this age'. Because of papal rulings, the consignment was sent through Customs marked expressly 'for His Most Christian Majesty' to avoid seizure. Such precautions were politically sound for a King bedevilled by the bastards of his predecessor.

Modern condoms are made from either latex rubber or the caecum (appendix) of a lamb. The two suppliers of skin condoms in the US get their supplies from slaughterhouses in New Zealand, the dried membranes being shipped in wooden boxes to Puerto Rico, where they are graded and have an elastic band glued to form a lip, using a glue developed during the First World War for balloonists who needed to repair the delicate skin of their craft.

Condom standards vary from country to country.

In Malaysia they must hold 5¼ pints (3 litres) of water to satisfy the Standards Institute. In Sweden, Canada and Holland, condoms are inflated until they burst, the Dutch standard requiring a condom to hold 6.6 gallons (25 litres) of air at a pressure of at least 0.9 kilopascals without bursting. The British, Indians and Israelis use a tensile test, stretching a sample of the latex from a condom until it breaks; new condoms must stretch by an average of 650 per cent and resist a force of 20 megapascals to comply.

The man who may have the largest collection of condoms in the world is Philip Kestelman, who worked with the International Planned Parenthood Federation for 15 years. One of the brands he was unable to procure was a Japanese condom, sold door-to-door in gross (144) packages designed to look like an encyclopaedia.

The word condom may derive from the name of Charles II's physician. The trade name Durex is an acronym of durable, reliable and excellent.

A 182-year-old French condom was sold at Christie's in London on 2 July 1992 for £3,300 ($4,700). The anonymous Scandinavian buyer planned to display it in a museum of erotica.

Thousands of foreign tourists visit the medieval French village of Condom in south-western France because they are amused by the town's name. The mayor Jacques Moizan says, 'If that's the reason they want to come to Condom, it doesn't bother me.'

Ozone, a gas which protects us from harmful ultra-violet radiation from the sun in the upper atmosphere, is also a pollutant when it is industrially created and occurs near the surface of the Earth. According to a 1992 experiment at the University College of

Los Angeles, it is also a danger to the integrity of condoms. After 72 hours' exposure to the gas at a level of 300 parts per billion – a level fairly standard in parts of southern California – only two out of 20 condoms tested remained intact; the others had become perforated and the tops had dropped off five.

FLOWERS

In 1986, President Reagan signed a bill declaring the rose the 'national floral emblem' of the USA, ending more than 70 attempts by Congress over a period of 20 years to resolve the matter. Other flowers under consideration had included daffodils, orange blossom, cornflowers and the marigold, the latter being advocated strongly for years by Senator Everett Dirksen until his death. Among the criteria for the emblem were that it had to be native to North America, attractive, easily propagated and recognized, grown in every state and possessing historical connections.

In 1982, the seeds of a lotus plant from a cache discovered in the 1920s in an ancient lakebed deposit in southern Manchuria were successfully germinated at the Agricultural University in Wageningen, the Netherlands.

In 1990, scientists at Yale University claimed that a fossil, previously thought to be a fern, is in fact a tiny flowering plant 120 million years old – five million years older than any previously identified flower.

The first black tulip to be revealed to the press in February 1986 was bred out of Queen of Night and Wienerwald by a Dutch bulb company, which had spent 25 years and at least £500,000 ($710,000) working on it.

202

The largest flower in the world is *Rafflesia arnoldii*, the extraordinary bloom of a highly specific fungal parasite that lives on only two species of grape vine found all over South-East Asia, from India to New Guinea. There are twelve species of *Rafflesia* but only *arnoldii* sports these enormous flowers, which can measure 3 feet (1 metre) across and weigh nearly 15 lbs (7 kgs), and are confined to the tropical forests of Sumatra.

The life cycle of this strange flower, which was first described in 1818 by Sir Stamford Raffles and his personal physician Joseph Arnold, is extraordinary. It begins life as fine thread-like structures within the host vine, which is stimulated to produce a cup-like structure on which the flowers are borne. They take two days to open and last only four to five days, during which time they are pollinated by carrion flies, attracted by their pungent smell. An enormous seed-bearing fruit is subsequently produced; it was confirmed by biologist Louise Emmons in 1991 that the seeds are dispersed by tree shrews and squirrels, who eat the pulpy flesh and excrete the seeds as they race up and down the vines that play host to these parasitic flowers.

Unfortunately, these flowers are threatened with extinction due to the destruction of their tropical forest habitat.

One hundred and thirteen years after its birth, Canada finally decided in 1980 that *O Canada* is its official national anthem.

The only known manuscript of *La Marseillaise*, written by Claude Joseph Rouget de l'Isle, on the night of 24 April 1792, was sold at an auction in Versailles in December 1981 to pop singer Serge Gainsbourg for 135,000 francs ($24,000). His successful bid was greeted by some boos and cat-calls from people annoyed by Gainsbourg's 1979 syncopated version. Originally conceived as a marching song for French troops on the Rhine, it was later adopted by the Marseilles Volunteers, whence came the name.

The tune of the British national anthem was first published as a national song in the *Thesaurus Magazine* of 1744. A year later, the *Gentleman's Magazine* published words to fit the tune, similar to those used today. The tune was then also adopted by the State of Vienna (1782), Prussia (1795) and Switzerland (1811). Sweden used it, and so did Russia until the revolution in 1917. The tune's origins are obscure. Some say it was composed by Henry Purcell, some by the musician John Bull. The tune also appears in works by Brahms, Beethoven, Haydn, Bach, Weber and Dvorak.

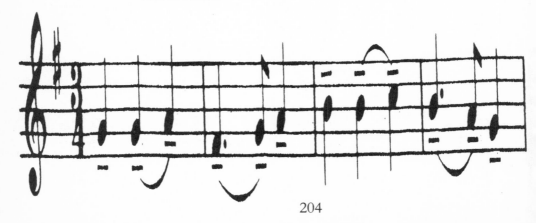

It is a criminal offence in the United States to alter the tune of *The Star-Spangled Banner*. Ivor Stravinsky almost landed in jail in the 1940s when he attempted to reorchestrate it. Rachmaninov prepared another unconventional version in 1918 for his first US tour as a Russian exile, but he was advised not to play it. It was recorded in 1982 by pianist Ian Hobson, who transcribed it from a piano roll of Rachmaninov himself playing the piece.

The words of the anthem were written on the back of an envelope by poet Francis Scott Key after witnessing the shelling in 1814 of Fort McHenry near Baltimore by the British fleet in Chesapeake Bay. Key, who had been sent to negotiate the release of a prisoner held by the British, was kept on board ship until the attack was over, and his words recall his feelings at the time. The 15-star, 15-stripe flag that was flown on that day and inspired Keys is now so decayed that the Smithsonian Institution only displays it to the public for two minutes every hour, so as to cut down further damage caused by light and dust.

That is the official story. But this is all baloney, according to P. William Filby, a former head of the Maryland Historical Society, which holds the oldest known copy of the poem. Filby began checking the facts of the story. For a start the flag, which measures 45 feet by 25 feet (14 metres x 7.6 metres), would have been sodden by rain, as there had been a gale the night before the attack; far from waving, it would more likely have been 'wrapped soggily around the pole'. Secondly, the envelope was not invented until 1840. He says the official version of the story has the day of composition and printing wrong, and that the tune comes from an eighteenth-century English drinking song, *Anacreon In Heaven*.

ROACH REMOVAL

The arrival at a Pittsburgh hospital of an unfortunate soul with a cockroach deep in each ear enabled doctors to test the two principal means of removal against each other. Into one ear they poured mineral oil – the little beast died slowly, and its corpse proved difficult to remove. Into the other ear they sprayed lidocaine anaesthetic aerosol – the unwanted lodger made a rapid escape and was summarily despatched with a shoe.

RANDI

James ('the Amazing') Randi uses his skills as a professional magician to travel the world exposing fraudulent phenomena.

Born in Toronto in 1928, Randall James Hamilton Zwinge was a precocious child. At the age of nine, he invented a pop-up toaster, and had mastered hieroglyphics, calculus and trigonometry by his early teens. By the time he was 17 he had left school and was touring, in a turban and a beard, as Prince Ibis, along with Kong Lee (the electric boy) and a 10-foot (3-metre) indigo snake. He graduated to the Canadian nightclub circuit as the Great Randall, and earned the name the Amazing Randi when he broke out of a locked police cell.

Z (THE LAND OF)

The land of Z is a 'fairly-well developed Third World country' invented by the US State Department and located in Virginia, where diplomats go for a 26-day course in order to experience foreign duty before tackling the real thing.

Amongst the problems they learn to deal with, through role-playing and other tests, are how to type out a passport and how to repatriate the bodies of

Americans who die abroad. The motto of the Land of Z is 'Money Conquers All'. Its major cities are Zrunchi, Zug, Zorrest, Ziff and Zeel. A briefing book issued to all new arrivals carries this brief warning: 'This is not the paradise you had envisioned.'

GUIDE DOGS

Dogs have served as protectors or guides for blind people for many centuries. The first modern work describing techniques for training guide dogs was published in Vienna in 1819, but the first guide dog training centre was not established until 1923 at Potsdam, Germany. The modern guide dog movement owes its development to Dorothy Harrison Eustis, a wealthy American woman living in Switzerland who visited Potsdam in 1927, wrote about it for the *Saturday Evening Post* and subsequently established *L'Oeil Qui Voit* (The Seeing Eye) in Switzerland and the US to train guide dogs.

Emma, a guide dog that went blind and had to be led around by another guide dog, won a gold medal for devotion to duty. It was presented at a dinner in London in December 1980.

An international conference of veterinary surgeons, held in London in April 1984, was told that the dogs most commonly used as guides for the blind (labradors, golden retrievers and German shepherd dogs) are more susceptible to blindness than other breeds.

Colour was unavailable to early firework-makers. When Handel wrote his *Music for the Royal Fireworks* in 1749 the only colours available were gold and silver. Colour emerged only in the nineteenth century as a by-product of new industrial techniques.

Black powder (the original gunpowder) was developed by the Chinese more than 1,000 years ago, travelled west during the Middle Ages and remains essentially unchanged today: a blend of potassium nitrate (saltpetre), charcoal and sulphur in a 75:15:10 ratio by weight.

According to Robert K.G. Temple in *China: Land of Discovery and Invention*, his popular account of extracts from the mammoth encyclopaedia of Chinese science compiled by Professor Joseph Needham: 'Gunpowder was invented in China not by people seeking better weapons or even explosives, but by alchemists seeking the elixir of immortality. What greater irony could there be than that men wishing to find a drug to enable them to live for ever should instead find a simple substance destined to kill millions of people?'

A few groups of molecules are responsible for nearly all the colours in fireworks. Compounds of the element strontium produce the reds, molecules containing barium create the greens, those containing sodium, the yellows. Blues, purples and violets are the hardest to create and are produced using copper chloride on its own or mixed with strontium chloride.

During a fireworks concert in Edinburgh in August 1985, a 15-inch (380-mm) shell packed with a 12-year-old-malt whisky was detonated high over Princes Street Gardens to produce a 'Scotch mist'.

Guy Fawkes was actually arrested on the night of November 4th and he was hung, drawn and quartered in January.

On 3 November 1990, a 120-foot (36.5-metre)-high replica of the Houses of Parliament was set alight by an electrician named Guy Fawkes at a party organized by the Torrington Cavaliers at Torrington in Devon to raise money for charity. Sixty other relatives of the original plotters were also present.

The most renowned of the world's firework competitions is an annual tournament held in Monte Carlo every summer. The entries, limited to five a year, are by invitation only and are drawn from the top class of firework companies, including Ogatsu of Japan, Ruggieri of France, Brunchu of Spain, and Fireworks by Grucci – an Italian-American clan involving 50 family members in the business.

Chinese fireworks have wonderful names including 'Moon Wooing Phoenix', 'Grapes all over the Vineyard' and 'Monkeys Violate the Heaven Palace'.

The last wish of Jeff Thorp, who died in April 1992, was that his ashes should be launched across the Cheshire Plain in 28 giant fireworks. After the successful ceremony in August that year, his widow commented: 'That's what Jeff wanted – to go out with a real bang, colouring the sunset with his ashes.'

Ideas as to how hailstones were formed remained purely theoretical until the work of two North American scientists, Lawrence Chang and David Rogers, was published in the *Journal of Atmospheric Science* in 1989.

A long-standing problem was that if hail forms by gradual accumulation around a water droplet or ice 'seed', how are the baby hailstones kept in one place long enough to grow in size before the strong updraughts in a storm cloud blow them away?

After catching hailstones in cone-shaped mosquito nets attached to bottles, comparing the different sizes and shapes and then relating them to radar maps and photos of the storm, the scientists came to the following conclusions.

Hailstones develop in small clouds at the edge of the storm, which act as breeding grounds. These clouds survive for about 20 minutes before being drawn into the main storm cloud. By then, the adolescent hailstones are heavy enough to avoid being swept away. Once the balance is lost, the hail falls.

In France, agricultural losses due to hailstones are estimated at £100 million ($142m) a year. In the Po Valley, the damage is even greater.

The *US Monthly Weather Review* of 1894 (Vol. 22, No. 215) reported that, on the afternoon of Friday 11 May, during a severe hailstorm at Vicksburg, a remarkably large hailstone was found to have a solid nucleus consisting of a piece of alabaster measuring half to three-quarters of an inch (13–19 mm). During the same storm, but eight miles to the east, a gopher turtle, measuring 6 by 8 inches (15 x 20 cms) and encased with ice, fell with the hail.

Nowhere is more heavily pelted with hail than the tea estates near Kericho and the Nandi Hills in Kenya, which have hail on 132 days a year on average. Intrigued as to why this should be so, Dr Russell Schnell and his wife Suan Neo Tan of the Environmental Research Laboratories in Boulder, Colorado, set out to investigate.

They discovered that the hailstorms may be seeded by the tea-pickers themselves, who stir up a large quantity of leaf litter in their activities. These particles are drawn up into the clouds and form the seeding agent around which the hailstones form.

Concorde was the first airliner to be certified to fly through hail.

UNIFORMS

President Nixon's views on this subject were epitomized in the special uniforms he ordered for the White House guards. Only worn once during his presidency, the uniforms consisted of white tunics, black gunbelts, visored caps, and yards of gold braid – more appropriate to Ruritania than Washington, DC. Following Nixon's demise, the uniforms gathered dust in a government warehouse – souvenirs which the Secret Service could not burn because destruction of Federal property is a crime.

In 1980 they were moved to Iowa Federal Surplus Division, attracting the attention of rock star Alice Cooper, who wanted to kit his roadies out in them for a concert celebrating the opening of his movie *Roadie*. The Secret Service said that the uniforms could not be used by private individuals. Instead they were given to the Southern Utah University as band uniforms on condition that the university would never 'sell, trade, lease, lend, bail, encumber, cannibalize, dismember or otherwise dispose of' them. Two of the band members appeared in uniform at one of Alice Cooper's concerts.

A design-a-uniform competition for the French army, with three prizes of 50,000 francs ($9,000), led to the following suggestions:
• Andres Courreges sketched a black soldier fitted out in sky blue, with tricolour braces, calf-high jungle boots, yellow socks and a baseball cap.
• Louis Feraud preferred uniforms decorated with embroidered flowers, gold buttons, and real blooms covering the helmet. Feraud admitted, 'I also like bow ties,' and commented that 'The army would be much more gay.'
• Michel Renoma favoured polo-neck pullovers, felt jackets with plenty of shoulder padding, tartan scarves, and brown leather laced cavalry boots.

ISLAND OF MENSTRUATING MEN

Wogeo is one of the largest of the Schouten Islands, (pronounced 'skowten') which lie 30 miles (48 kms) off the north coast of Papua New Guinea. The neighbouring inhabited islands are called Koil, Blupblup, Kadovar and Bam (so named because its active volcano is in constant eruption).

Wogeo is also known as the Island of Menstruating Men, in a curious anthropological study carried out by Australian Professor Ian Hogbin, who lived there for the whole of 1934, returning for a few weeks in 1948.

In Wogeo society, men and women 'face one another in more or less balanced opposition'. It is held that 'The members of each sex group would be

212

safe and invulnerable, healthy and prosperous, if only they were to keep to themselves and refrain from mixing with members of the other sex group.'

This obviously proves impossible in practice. Females are fortunate in that menstruation regularly frees them from contamination – 'The alien elements flow away of their own accord.' Men must regain their purity by artificial menstruation, an operation known as *baras*, the word that is used for a woman having a period.

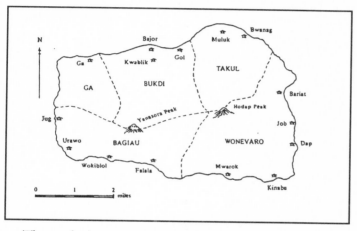

The technique a man uses is to catch a crayfish or crab, remove one of its claws, and keep it wrapped in ginger; he then collects soothing leaves and a fruit with a deep purple skin. From dawn of that day he eats nothing. Late in the afternoon he finds a lonely beach and cuts his penis deeply on both sides of the glans with the claw to produce profuse bleeding. The blood must not touch his fingers or his legs. Afterwards he wraps his penis in the leaves, returns to the village and recuperates for several days.

This is known to be a good cure for sickness and must be re-enacted on a regular basis. Hogbin records: 'Warriors make sure to menstruate before setting out on a raid, traders before carving an overseas canoe or refurbishing its sails, hunters before weaving a new net for trapping pigs.'

HICCUPS

Charlie Osborne of Anthon, Iowa, has been hiccupping since 1922. The only thing that helps is three daily teaspoons of damson plum preserve, which slows his hiccup rate down from 40 hics a minute to 20. One doctor has a theory that Osborne broke a small blood vessel at the base of his brain while lifting a huge pig on his farm. His affliction has not prevented him from marrying twice and fathering eight children.

West German Heinz Isecke began hiccupping after a stomach operation in 1973. For two years doctors tried every treatment known, including electric shock treatment and an operation to cut the nerves that control the diaphragm. It was no use. He had to sell his plumbing business and lost 4 stone (25 kgs) in weight.

In 1975, Herr Isecke committed suicide by jumping out of a second-storey hospital window, after an estimated 36 million spasms. He had previously attempted suicide by taking an overdose of sleeping tablets.

Pope Pius X suffered from hiccups for 12 years and 242 days.

Why people hiccup remains a mystery, but hiccups may be the last vestige of some primitive protective reflex. They are caused when the nerves leading to the diaphragm become irritated, sending it into spasms. The vagus nerve in the ear is associated with the hiccup reflex, as is the phrenic nerve, which travels from the diaphragm to the neck.

One-fifth of hiccups cases are triggered by emotional stress or anxiety; the percentage may be more than four times as high among women, but hiccups occur far more frequently among men.

Persistent hiccups may be a symptom of serious illnesses. In the early 1900s there were mass hiccup outbreaks in Winnipeg in Canada, connected with flu and encephalitis epidemics. This suggests that a viral element may be involved.

Cures for hiccups are legion and include using cannabis, hypnosis, acupuncture, tranquillizers and electrical stimulation. Plato recommended a thump on the back.

AMBER

Amber is prehistoric tree resin that has been transmuted over millions of years, by processes not yet fully understood, into fossil form. It is found in many parts of the world, from Alaska to the Lebanon, but the two main sources are the Baltic region (Denmark, Germany, Poland, Russia) and the Dominican Republic, where it is mined commercially.

Long prized for its 'magical' property of acquiring electricity when rubbed (the Greek word for amber is *elektron*), amber is collected not only for its beauty, but also because of its scientific value.

Thousands of small organisms and insects are found trapped in amber, many in remarkable states of preservation, raising the possibility of extracting DNA from fossil nuclei for study.

Many relationships between long-dead organisms are fixed for all time in amber, allowing scientists to study not only midges but the mites that ride on their backs (a symbiotic association known as phoresis). Nematodes have been preserved in amber as they emerged from the abdomens of ants some 25 million years ago.

The oldest DNA in the world yet found was in the tissues of stingless bees entrapped in amber between 25 and 40 million years ago.

Born in a well-to-do family in Strasburg, a prodigy who was doing adult drawing by the age of ten, Gustave Doré is considered to be the ancestor of the comic strip.

By the age of 22 he had already published 700 drawings, and five albums of artwork, and he remained energetic and inventive until his death. Working at fantastic speed, he drew directly on to wood-blocks but even at this rate it took him three years to complete his illustrations for Dante's *Inferno*. Other works included Rabelais's *Gargantua* and *Pantagruel*, Peurrault's *Fairy Tales* and *Don Quixote*.

In 1868 he arrived in London and hired a large gallery in Bond Street to display his work. Two and a half million people came in over a 20-year period. The gallery is now the sale rooms of Sotheby's.

His greatest work, a lavish edition of Coleridge's *Ancient Mariner*, was a commercial disaster; his home city of Strasburg was lost to Germany after the Franco-Prussian War; and his adored mother died.

He shut himself up in Paris and began a new career as a sculptor. His biggest work was the memorial to Alexandre Dumas in the Place Malesherbes in Paris. Entirely self-taught, he became Sarah Bernhardt's teacher.

Doré died in 1883 at the age of 51 of a heart attack. In his career he had illustrated over 200 books – some with 4–500 plates – made over 100 lithographs and etchings, painted 280 watercolours and done 500 original drawings. Add to that 100 paintings of a quality high enough to prolong a one-man show over 20 years, and 50 pieces of sculpture. His total graphic output amounted to more than 10,000 works.

He was working on Poe's *The Raven* when he died and much of his work suggests psychological unease.

Vincent Van Gogh, then an obscure artist, wrote

in a letter to a friend, 'When those who cannot do with their ten fingers a tenth of what Doré can do with one revile his work, then it's nothing but humbug.'

MUNCHAUSENS

Sufferers from Munchausen's Syndrome have a compulsive habit of seeking medical attention for either fictitious or self-inflicted ailments.

The condition is named after Baron Karl Friedrich Hieronymous von Münchausen (1720–97), a German army officer whose boasts about his battlefield heroics provided the basis for a humorous bestseller and made his name a byword for preposterous tales.

One common type of Munchausen consists of people who are addicted to the surgeon's knife. They will happily swallow foreign objects or injure themselves in order to undergo an operation.

A fish porter regularly swallowed 50p (70-cent) pieces in order to be admitted to hospital and be looked after by friendly nurses. He told magistrates that the trick had worked more than 70 times.

Most hospitals now keep 'black books' listing known bogus patients, like the woman who rushed into the emergency ward with a frighteningly high temperature. It was later discovered that she'd been drawing blood from her arm, mixing it with salad cream, and reinjecting it.

One of the worst cases concerned a six-year-old girl from Yorkshire, England, who was in hospital 12 times, during which she underwent six examinations under anaesthetic, several major X-ray tests, unpleasant drug treatments, and had her urine analysed 150 times. Only after 16 consultants had given their opinions was it discovered that the girl was perfectly healthy. Her mother had been tampering with the urine samples and falsifying her symptoms.

ZAR

In the Sudan *Zar* healing is a very ancient form of mental treatment, based on the theory that the atmosphere is full of good and evil spirits (the Zars) waiting to enter a person.

A Zar healer must identify which kind of Zar the sick person has and either replace it with a more suitable one, or reconcile the person to living with the Zar he has. Zars can enter the patient under varied circumstances such as after childbirth or an accident, or after a person has broken the moral law. There are 'doctor' Zars, 'Abyssinian' Zars, 'child-killing' Zars, 'leopard' Zars – even 'English' Zars.

After long discussions with the patient, the healer will then stage a casting-out ceremony that may last two days, with the patient repeatedly dancing to exhaustion, followed by the ceremonial killing of an animal. Depending on the patient's financial circumstances, the animal chosen ranges from a chicken to a camel, and the patient is covered with its blood.

SEX

More than one million acts of sexual intercourse take place every day, according to calculations by the World Health Organisation. They result in 910,000 conceptions and 356,000 incidences of sexually transmitted disease.

AIR-CONDITIONING

Houston is the most air-conditioned place on Earth. The cost of turning its hot air into cold air exceeds the gross national product of 30 countries.

An accidental city founded on a swamp which now has a population of 1.6 million people, Houston is one of the hottest cities in the States and, for six months of the year, the most humid.

Houston Lighting and Power claims that the cooling capacity of all the city's air conditioners is 3.5 million tonnes, and homeowners and businesses spend some $666 million on electricity to run them during the 'cooling season' from May to October.

The telephone book contains 63 pages related to the air-conditioning business, including 700 licensed contractors. More than 50 of the city's downtown buildings are linked by a 3-mile (4.8-km) network of air-conditioned tunnels.

Houston is also sinking into the swamp on which it stands; it is expected to subside 14 inches (35.5 cms) by the year 2020.

UNKNOWN WARRIOR

The grave of the Unknown Warrior in Westminster Abbey contains the body of a British soldier from one of the four main battle areas of the First World War – the Aisne, the Somme, Arras and Ypres. On the night of 7 November 1920 a body from each was taken to the Chapel of St Pol, and one of the unidentified corpses was selected by Brigadier-General Wyatt to be placed in a coffin sent from England. (The other bodies were reburied in a military cemetery.) This coffin was placed inside another of English oak, bound with wrought-iron bands through which a crusader's sword from the Tower of London was passed. The destroyer HMS *Verdun* carried it to England, and on 11 November the body was laid to rest in the Abbey, on earth brought from Ypres, and was covered with a slab of black Belgian marble from a quarry near Namur.

It is the only grave in the Abbey which is never walked over.

Louwrens van Voorthuizen was a Dutch fisherman until 1950, when he declared himself to be God and assembled a small band of devoted followers known as 'Lou-men' and 'Lou-women'. He preached that traditional Christianity was obsolete now that God had returned to Earth, and rejected all forms of conventional morality. He was passionately fond of cigars, and justified his habit by asking, 'Why shouldn't God smoke?' He died in 1968.

The Muggletonians were a religious sect founded in 1652 by two London tailors, John Reeve and Ludowick Muggleton. They claimed that God had visited them and told them they were 'the last two witnesses of the spirit' described in the Book of Revelation. They were instructed to announce doomsday and declare the true faith.

Reeve died four years later but the sect continued to follow the Divine Commission received by its two prophets. Thereafter membership steadily declined, and the last Muggletonian died in 1979.

In his book *Strange Sects and Cults*, Egon Larsen records the existence of the following:

• The Electricity Culture Religion, which elevated Thomas Alva Edison to the status of a god.

• A sect called the Four Square Gospel, led by Mrs Aimee Semple MacPherson, an American revivalist prophet of the 1920s. It boasted 'a brass band bigger and louder than Sousa's, a female choir bigger and more beautiful than the Metropolitan

Opera chorus, and a costume wardrobe comparable to Ziegfelds'.

• The Essene cult, an early variety of Judaism, which worshipped dogs. They believed that there was a King Dog at the time of Christ, and that it died on the day of the Crucifixion. At the end of Christ's thousand-year reign, another King Dog will appear, and with him the Kingdom of Heaven. Departed souls are accompanied on the road to heaven by dogs.

The Church of the Sub-Genius numbers William Burroughs, David Byrne and Robert Crumb among its 30,000 followers. A mail-order church, its followers worship a pipe-smoking travelling salesman named J.R. 'Bob' Dobbs, who speaks to aliens and on whose 'wheelings and dealings' the fate of the world depends. He teaches that 'LOVE IS THE ANSWER — THE LOVE OF MONEY'.

Founded by film editor Doug Smith, a.k.a. Rev. Stang, whose obsessive hobby is 'crackpotology', the church urges its followers to attain 'Slack' — total happiness and freedom — which we are prevented from reaching by a conspiracy of 'Normals'. Stang claims that 'Bob doesn't blame us for our sins. He came here to justify them.'

CHEWING-GUM

The raw material that gives chewing-gum its chewiness is chicle, which comes from the sapodilla trees of Central America. The men who collect it are called *chicleros*, and spend up to eight months a year living in workcamps in the jungle.

A sapodilla tree takes between 50 and 80 years to reach maturity, and it should be 20 years old at least before it is 'tapped' for chicle. It can then be tapped five or six times before it dies. The liquid sap is collected in leather pouches, boiled, poured into a wooden mould and marked with an official stamp. Mules transport it out of the forest.

The origins of chewing-gum can be traced to 1845, when a 30-lb (13.6-kg) ball of chicle latex was the sole asset of Santa Anna, the former Caudillo of Mexico and conqueror of the Alamo, who was in exile on Staten Island, New York. He hoped to earn a fortune by developing chicle as a rubber substitute and gave it to the inventor Thomas Adams, Sr to investigate its possibilities. Adams was unable to vulcanize it for use in tyres, but the chicle chewing-gum balls he sent to a friend who was a druggist in New Jersey sold out immediately. Santa Anna died in poverty but Adams made a fortune, and the corporation founded in his name still makes Chiclets.

Chewing things has a long history. In the Middle East people still chew gum from the mastic tree, and the Greek *mastikhao* (to chew) gave us the word 'masticate'. People have chewed ginseng, betel nuts, blubber, tobacco, spruce gum and paraffin wax.

The major brands of Wrigley's chewing-gum were introduced as follows: Juicy Fruit (1893), Doublemint (1893), Spearmint (1914). William J. Wrigley, Jr began by offering his gum free with soap powder, and chewing-gum made and lost him three fortunes.

Singapore has banned chewing-gum. Culture Minister Mr Suppiah Dhanabalan claimed that it was costing £50,000 ($71,000) annually to remove it from floors and walls.

During the Second World War, General MacArthur bought up the entire production of Wrigley's in Australia and dropped it over the Japanese-occupied Philippines. It came in a special wrapper bearing the slogan 'I shall return – MacArthur'.

Buster Keaton was born in the tiny town of Pickway, Kansas, on 4 October 1895. The story goes that, at the age of six months, the young Keaton fell down a flight of stairs at the theatrical boarding-house where his parents were staying. By chance, another member of the troupe, the then unknown Harry Houdini, witnessed the accident. He rushed over and was surprised to find the boy not only unharmed but laughing. When he told the parents, he said, 'That's some buster your baby took.' The name stuck.

Buster first appeared on stage at the age of nine months, and by the age of seven he was a regular part of the family act, The Three Keatons. This involved a nightly violent physical routine with his father, made funny by the fact that Buster never smiled. After a few years this became automatic, and his trademark – 'The Great Stone Face' – was born.

The Navigator, Buster's first real popular success, had an unusual genesis. Keaton heard that a 500-foot (150-metre) ocean liner, the SS *Buford,* was headed for the wreckers, so he bought it for $25,000. The film was conceived around it.

His most famous acquisition was a 'land yacht', purchased from the Pullman Company and built by the Fifth Avenue coach company in New York. Keaton was the admiral of this strange craft, which was 30 feet (9 metres) long, with a dining room and a kitchen, and two bedrooms to sleep six. Dressed in nautical costumes from the MGM props department, with actor friend Lew Cody as vice-admiral and manservant Willy Caruthers as chauffeur, Keaton would set out on extended trips, which were spoken of as real sea voyages. The correct nautical language was used at all times.

Samuel Beckett wrote *Waiting for Godot* with Keaton in mind.

QUETELET

Adolphe Quetelet, a nineteenth-century Belgian statistician, was the first to record that children are not born at the same rate throughout the day. The peak in births occurs towards the end of the night and in the early morning; the trough in the early afternoon. Quetelet also pioneered the use of statistics by governments, and was the first to present the statistical concept of the 'average man' in *On Man* (1835).

DISSECTORS

The two earliest jigsaw-puzzle-makers, known as 'dissectors', were John Spilsbury and William Darton. Their shops were virtually next door to each other in London in the late eighteenth century.

The first 'dissections' were of maps, and thereby hangs a tale. Daniel Wheeler, a Quaker, believed that God wanted him to undertake a mission, but he knew not where – until, that is, he noticed a piece of his children's dissected map lying apart from the rest, St Petersburg. He went there and sat out a long cold winter, waiting for the call. Sure enough, Tsar Alexander asked for his help with a drainage scheme for the city and, as a result, 3,000 acres (1,215 hectares) of marsh and swamp were reclaimed. There is a monument to Wheeler outside St Petersburg to this day.

VELCRO

Velcro was invented by Georges de Mestral, (1907–1990), a prolific Swiss inventor. While out hunting in 1941, he became fascinated by the burrs of the burdock weed sticking to his clothing and his dog's coat. Microscopic examination of their structure led him to the idea of duplicating it, using man-made materials, and Velcro was born.

It took him 14 years to patent and de Mestral did not open his first factory until 1957. Now enough Velcro ribbon is produced each year to run twice round the world.

Velcro was used on the spacesuits of the astronauts who landed on the moon in 1969 and to fix objects inside the cabin of the *Apollo* spacecraft. (A patch of Velcro is fixed inside astronauts' helmets so they can scratch their noses.) It has also been used to hold together the pumping chambers of artificial hearts and the thermal insulation blanket between Concorde's outer and inner fuselage. General Motors have tested Velcro as a back-up support structure for car bumpers, as the loop's strength increases under vibration.

In 1988 researchers at Velcro's New Hampshire headquarters announced perhaps their most significant breakthrough – silent Velcro, in which noise levels are reduced by 95 per cent in answer to a request from the US Army.

De Mestral was also the first man to propose the ideas of fibre optics and plastic shotgun cartridges and he developed a commercially successful asparagus peeler before he died.

HALCYON DAYS

According to Roger Tory Peterson: 'The mythical halcyon, the kingfisher, was rumoured to lay its eggs on the quiet waters of the sea, hence the lovely term "halcyon days".' Kingfishers actually nest in burrows in river banks.

UTOPIA

Utopia now officially exists. It was the name given to the landing site on Mars for the spacecraft *Viking 2*.

MAPS

In *The Image*, Kenneth Boulding writes: 'It has been seriously suggested that the history of World War I was profoundly affected by the fact that in school atlases of the old German Empire, the United States and Germany each occupied a single page. This led to a serious underestimate on the part of the Germans of the size and capacity of the United States.'

In 1913, Charles Trowbridge, a pioneer of the concept of 'mental maps', noted that some people seemed to be able to navigate well in cities and had a good sense of orientation, while others got confused. They used imaginary maps in their heads, centred on their homes. He recommended directional training for children in schools.

He justified his work: 'the matter has a pertinent relation to the training of children to become soldiers . . . It would appear necessary that children should be seated at school in a special manner when studying geography, the cardinal points of the compass marked in the room, and the maps in the books properly oriented and the imaginary maps systematically corrected in childhood.'

The widely-used Mercator map projection, drawn in 1569 by the Flemish cartographer Gerardus Mercator, exaggerates the size of Greenland 16 times, making it appear bigger than South America when, in fact, it is only about the size of Mexico.

It was designed to satisfy the navigators' demands for a chart on which compass courses could be laid down as straight lines. As a result, lines of latitude get further apart as they move towards the poles.

A 1988 Gallup poll in the US showed that three out of ten Americans cannot distinguish north from south on a map.

On 16 December 1988, the Australian federal government announced that, after 23 years and the expenditure of £300 million ($425m), the entire continent had finally been recorded on topographic maps for the first time.

In the USA, the task of measuring the country in minute detail, begun in 1883 by one-armed Civil War veteran John Wesley Powell, will not be completed until the end of the century. By 1983 the US Geological Survey had completed 82 per cent of the country at a scale of one inch to 2,000 feet (25 mm to 7.6 metres), twice as detailed as Powell's maps. The Survey employs only 1,850 people, compared to 4,000 employees at the Ordnance Survey in Britain, and they have a saying around the office that 'Only a country as rich as ours can afford to be so poorly mapped.'

ZHANG

In the Western world there are a vast number of surnames and a relatively limited number of first names. It is the reverse in China.

The supply of first names (which are actually second names because the surname is put first) is infinite, being created on a do-it-yourself basis — 'maintain security', 'green piano', 'jade bell', 'benefit the country' are some examples, in translation.

If all the people surnamed Zhang in China were to secede and set up their own state, it would be the world's eighth most populous nation in the world with 100 million people.

BITING

After examining injury reports from hospitals in New York City, Dr John S. Marr, an assistant health commissioner, and two medical colleagues discovered that, in 1977, more people were bitten by other people than were bitten by rodents – 892 compared with 229. The figures for 1978 were 763 (people-bites) to 249 (rodents) and for 1979 they were 973 to 233.

Dr Marr claims that people-bites attack 'almost every part of the body' and that the bites increase in early summer, perhaps because victims wear less pro-

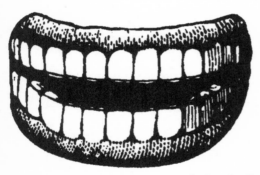

tective clothing. These injuries are 'a serious medical and surgical problem' because, Dr Marr observes, 'The human mouth is a pretty dirty place.'

People biting people is always news. The *Curious Facts* archives bulge with stories of rugby players biting off each other's ears, and footballers biting the ears off referees; other vulnerable professions are nurses, police, taxi drivers, burglars and traffic wardens. Lovers' tiffs are common, with lost tongues a familiar complaint. Here are two of the most curious stories:

On 8 July 1977, Associated Press reported that a jobless worker had bitten the ear off an official at the employment office in Koldby, Denmark, and left it on the counter wrapped in paper with the message 'This is your ear.' Doctors later sewed it back on, but told him it would probably never be quite the same.

In 1985, a police sergeant in Montreal told a court that he had been bitten by a nun belonging to the Apostles of Infinite Love sect, when he tried to arrest her for soliciting donations without a permit.

In his work, *Dental Identification and Forensic Odontology*, Warren Harvey relates a case in which the tip of a finger, bitten from an attacker, carried enough fingerprints to lead to an arrest.

MAN BITES DOG is considered the ultimate newspaper story. Reuters reported one such incident on 30 June 1977, which took place at Blankenberge, Belgium. A dog-owner tried to stop a fight between his small mongrel and a four-year-old setter by biting the setter himself. He stopped when the setter's owner hit him over the head with her handbag. The man was charged with assault. The setter suffered severe bite wounds and a broken rib.

Reuters reported in December 1986 that a French teenager had been given a three-month suspended sentence and fined 3,000 francs ($530) for trying to bite a policeman when her Alsatian dog refused to do so.

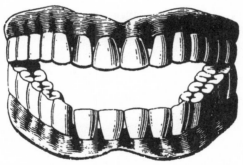

In 1982, the Hebrew newspaper *Yediot Ahronot* reported that a man arrested in Tel Aviv for biting his wife told police he dreamt he was a dog. The 73-year-old man hurt his wife so badly she had to receive hospital treatment.

The 'biting bandit' terrorized the town of Homestead, 20 miles (32 kms) south-west of Miami. In six attacks he gnawed the cheeks, ears and fingers of his victims whilst robbing them. He chewed off the finger of one victim to get at a ring.

In Victorian times, the magazine *Punch* advised all travellers to include in their luggage the *Railway Pocket Companion,* which contained 'a small bottle of water, a tumbler, a complete set of surgical instruments, a packet of lint, and directions for making a will.'

The Hungarian Sylvestre Matuschka stated at his trial that his profession was that of a 'train wrecker'. Matuschka experienced sexual excitement most deeply when he saw a train crashing. He claimed that this had been induced by a hypnotist at a fair.

On New Year's Day 1931, he attempted without success to derail the Vienna–Passau train. On 8 August the same year, 16 passengers were injured when he succeeded in derailing the Vienna express near Berlin. On 12 September he caused the Bia–Torbagy express disaster, in which 22 people died.

Matuschka attempted to sue Hungarian Railways, claiming to be a victim of the very disaster he was responsible for. A map was found at his home with further disasters marked in red ink – he had planned one a month. After a series of trials he was hanged in 1934.

Hitler employed 100 officials and 80 engineers on secret plans for a transcontinental railway. The engines were to be 183 feet 7 inches (56 metres) long and have 52 axles; they were to pull huge double-decker carriages 22 feet 5 inches (6.8 metres) high by 19 feet 8 inches (6 metres) wide and travel at speeds of up to 155 mph (250 km/h).

The secret plans were discovered by accident in the 1970s by Anton Joachimsthaler, who published a full account of their history for the first time in 1982.

In 1976 Mr Ernest Digweed, a retired teacher from Portsmouth, left £26,100 ($37,000) net in trust in his will to be paid to 'the Lord Jesus Christ' in the event of a Second Coming. The will states that the money should be invested for 80 years: 'If during those eighty years the Lord Jesus Christ shall come to reign on Earth, then the Public Trustees, upon obtaining proof which shall satisfy them of his identity, shall pay to the Lord Jesus Christ all the property which they hold on his behalf.' The accumulated interest on the money is to go to the Crown after 21 years. The will further states that if Jesus doesn't show up by the end of the 80-year period, the Crown gets it all.

Tom Baggs died laughing. A former war correspondent who made a fortune in advertising in America, he died at the age of 84 in 1973 and left £45,000 ($64,000) to Birmingham University – where he had studied for a degree in English – to discover what makes people happy. The money financed a series of Baggs Memorial Lectures 'on the subject of happiness – what it is and how it may be achieved by individuals as well as nations'.

Mrs Kathleen Edwards of Southall, Middlesex, who died in May 1984, stated in her will: 'I would like my funeral car to stop outside The Plough public house, Norwood Green, so my husband can have his usual pint. I will wait as I have always waited.'

Born in Boston of Polish descent, Korczak Ziolkowski first discovered he had a talent for carving while working as an apprentice pattern-maker at a shipyard. Without any formal training he developed his talents and became a noted sculptor.

In 1939 he worked as chief assistant to Gutzon Borglum on the four giant heads of US Presidents Washington, Lincoln, Jefferson and Roosevelt, which comprise the Mount Rushmore Memorial and provided a fitting backdrop for the climax of Hitchcock's *North By Northwest*.

Ziolkowski was subsequently approached by Henry Standing Bear, a nephew of Crazy Horse, the warrior who had led the Sioux at the Battle of Little Big Horn in 1876, and asked if he would carve an equally impressive monument to this great Sioux warrior, who was bayoneted to death in army custody.

In 1949 Ziolkowski began work at Thunderhead Mountain in the Black Hills, which are sacred to the Sioux. Refused a government grant, he sold his property in Connecticut, built a log home for his family at the base of the mountain and constructed a 700-foot (213-metre) stairway to the rock face.

The statue will be colossal when completed – a 641-foot (195-metre)-long, 563-foot (172-metre)-high three-dimensional rendering of the chief astride his war pony. Four thousand people could stand on his outstretched arm; all four Mount Rushmore heads could fit inside the head of Crazy Horse. A five-room house would fit comfortably in the flaring nostril of his pony.

Ziolkowski shifted seven million tonnes of rock before he died in 1982 at the age of 74 after surviving two heart attacks, slipping five discs and being struck by a 300-lb (136-kg) cable. He is buried at the base of the mountain, and his work is being continued by his wife and eight of his ten children.

Bezoar stones are not stones at all but concretions of partially digested and calcified hair found in the alimentary canals of goats, antelopes and other ruminants. For centuries it was claimed that they had a mysterious power to purify wine poisoned with arsenic. Most valued in the Renaissance was the 'true' stone that came from the bezoar goat, whose Persian name means 'to protect against poison'. Queen Elizabeth I wore them set in silver. Napoleon was given a set by the Shah of Persia but, considering them worthless, threw them in the fire.

The legend has now been scientifically proved – in part, at least – by Andrew Benson, working at the Scripps Institution of Oceanography in the US. He observed tropical algae that were able to absorb arsenate (a derivative of arsenic), transform it into arsenite (arsenic's second toxic form) and then neutralize this by combining it with sulphur in the algae's protein. The hair protein in bezoar stones is broken down during its journey through the animal's gut, exposing building sites where sulphur acts similarly as a 'chemical sponge' for arsenite, neutralizing its effect. It is still not clear whether the reaction occurs quickly enough to detoxify a goblet of wine by simply immersing the stone in it.

In 1983, the journal *Gastroenterology* contained an Israeli report on an outbreak of gastro-intestinal bezoars in humans. Doctors were staggered when, in just five months, 71 Israelis had to have bezoars surgically removed. The cause was found to be unripe persimmons eaten by the patients, all of whom had surgery for ulcers. The fruit released a soluble tannin that coagulated with body acids to form a sticky mass, gluing together the seeds and pulp of the fruit into a lump that was further compressed by the intestines.

In 1988 a 35-year-old man from Kansas City was admitted to the Truman Medical Center complaining of stomach pains and internal bleeding. The source of the problem proved to be a 3-inch (8-cm)-long egg-shaped bezoar made of polystyrene. The patient admitted he enjoyed eating Styrofoam cups (a condition doctors dubbed polystyrenomania), but the question remained as to how such a bezoar was created. The theory is that butterfats in the stomach broke down the bonds of the polystyrene molecules and that the stomach muscles pressured it into a ball as hard as glass.

PARROTS

Parrots should be viewed as 'flying primates' due to their intelligence and the complexity of their social life. One African grey named Alex, studied for 12 years by Irene Pepperberg of Illinois's Northwestern University, can categorize objects according to colour, shape or material and understand other abstract concepts at a level previously discovered only in primates. Parrots as pets require as much attention as human toddlers, otherwise they become bored, frustrated and depressed. They are incredibly social birds, permanently attached to one partner, and have a preference for manipulating food with their left foot, which may be comparable to right-handedness in humans. This may link in to the parrot's linguistic skills.

234

Axl the parakeet was due to make his national television début on Johnny Carson's *Tonight Show* in May 1990, but a few hours before the performance his owner, David Cota, returned to his hotel room in Los Angeles to find that his room-mate had fallen asleep and had rolled over on Axl, also asleep on the bed, crushing him to death.

Csoki (pronounced Choky) is an African grey parrot with red tail feathers, who was left £10,000 ($14,200) in the will of her late owner, Victoria Brown of Hampstead, when she died in December 1989. She is cared for at a sanctuary in East Sussex by Stanley Hall, who has more than 20 of the birds. He looked after Alec Guinness's parrot, which the actor had taught to repeat four lines of a sonnet. It escaped and went missing for days until Hall heard it reciting the sonnet and traced it to the edge of a fox hole. When he picked it up it fainted. Hall recalls: 'It was inside my shirt and we were watching television together when it died.'

An estimated 77 of the world's 330 species of parrot are in immediate danger of extinction. The scarlet macaw *(Ara Macao)* is among the world's most threatened birds.

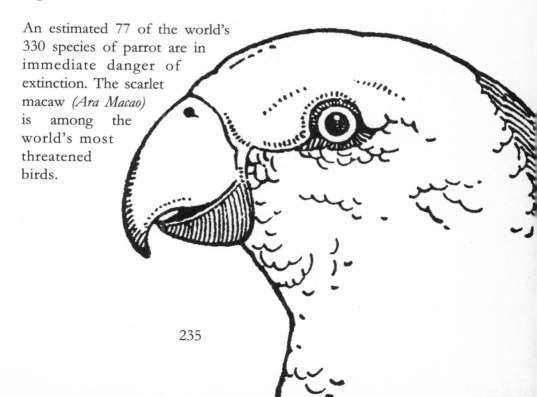

EXPLOSIVE SURGERY

In May 1980, a Chinese surgeon used a 'miniature bomb' inserted in the gall bladder of a 40-year-old worker to break up a gallstone. The report from the New China News Agency claimed that the patient felt only slight vibration and numbness. A doctor and an explosives expert set off more than 100 experimental explosions before working out the right dosage.

A new treatment for kidney stones was invented by the German aerospace company Dornier, a spin-off from their aerodynamic research. The device, called an extra-corporeal shock-wave lithotripter, creates loud shock waves, which pass through the body and shatter the stones into fragments that can then be passed out cleanly in the urine.

Patients are strapped in a chair and lowered into a metal tub full of water. X-ray scanners locate the stone and the chair is manoeuvred into the right position. A spark plug on the floor of the bath is fired, this creates a pressure wave and the sound is passed by a metal reflector on to the stone. The patient feels only a slight punch.

The makers claim it is effective in 85 per cent of cases. It cannot deal with two to five per cent of the stones, which are made of hard cystine; large stones called staghorns, because they have been moulded by the kidney's branching cavities, may also be a problem because, once broken, they create so much debris they may dam up the kidney's exit.

Corporal Mario Oliviera was 22 years old when he was hit by a 15-inch (38-mm) M-60 rifle grenade in a clash with Namibian guerrillas. The missile penetrated his lungs but became lodged in his rib-cage with its fins sticking out of his chest. The unstable nature of the live grenade meant that

236

the field hospital had to be evacuated and a barricade erected round the patient before the operation could start.

A doctor inserted a hot needle into the plastic fin, tied a wire into this and, using a pulley, slowly pulled out the missile, which was taken to a safe distance and detonated. Oliviera survived.

It is not generally known that President Reagan was shot with an exploding bullet in the assassination attempt on him in 1981, but that it failed to explode. Surgeons had to take special precautions when operating, since even the use of ultrasound or microwave diagnostic techniques could have set it off.

The *New England Journal of Medicine* carried a report in 1983 of an explosive operation on a heart patient, who had previously been fitted with a 'patch' of nitroglycerin, which is used in the treatment of heart disease. The drug is administered in this way so that it diffuses through the skin over a sustained period. The patient in this case had a heart attack and doctors tried to save him by giving him an electric shock. The result was a loud bang, a flash and a puff of yellow smoke. The patient was not damaged by the explosion, but died of the heart attack.

A 26-year-old Dane died on the operating table when an electrically heated surgical knife caused his stomach to explode.

Dr Niels Jentoft Olsen and Dr Vagn Berg, writing in the weekly journal of the Danish Medical Association, said the knife had burned through the patient's digestive tract wall and ignited explosive gases. The explosion was so violent that part of the colon was completely destroyed. In spite of further operations to repair the damage, the patient died of blood poisoning.

During the 1979 season in Yosemite National Park in California, campers left behind the following, according to the Environmental News Service: six human skeletons, 487 pairs of glasses, three car bodies, including a 1952 Nash Rambler, 16 toupees, four full wigs, two plastic statues of Jesus, 123 tape cassettes, five tape recorders, two TV sets, 22 cameras, 41 sleeping bags, 4,028 lipstick dispensers, a bathtub, a telephone, four typewriters, two church pews with cushions and more than 10,000 combs.

In 1977, 12 people were killed in Hong Kong by garbage that fell or was thrown from tall buildings, according to a government report.

A sect of Coptic Christians, landless labourers who migrated to the capital in the 1930s, the 25,000-strong Zabbaleens are the rubbish barons of Cairo. They operate the only household garbage collection system in the city and work seven days a week, ten hours a day for no pay. Their only reward is the refuse itself. Routes are handed down from father to son and the whole system is run by a group of Muslims called the Wahiya, or bosses, who contract with tenants and landlords to collect the rubbish, then sell the rights to the Zabbaleen to pick it up and keep it, charging both sides about 50 cents a month for a luxury apartment. The service costs the city nothing.

The garbage project has been running at the University of Arizona since 1973, under the direction of William Rathje, America's best-known garbologist.

By applying archaeological techniques and principles to the study of American trash, Rathje and colleagues have come up with valuable information and fresh insights.

For instance, consistent analysis of the garbage from certain selected Tucson neighbourhoods shows that the city's 400,000 inhabitants throw out 26 tonnes of food every night, of which one-third are plate scrapings. Projections from these figures suggest that Americans as a nation discard 10,000 tonnes of food a day, or 3.6 million tonnes a year.

Garbage project workers have also regularly bored into nine landfill sites throughout the US and discovered that disposable diapers, fast-food packaging and expanded polystyrene foam – three items which most people surveyed believed would take up at least 70 per cent of each landfill – actually constituted only three per cent of landfill volume. The biggest single contributor to landfills they discovered was paper, which makes up 40 per cent, of which 13 per cent is taken up by newspapers. Plastics account for 12 per cent of landfill waste and building waste a further 20 per cent.

Furthermore, the rubbish in modern landfills hardly rots, because they are too well sealed and are thus too dry. In 1987, he discovered a 1982 head of lettuce, dated by the newspapers nearby it, in the Fresh Kills landfill in New York, which looked better than many do after a week in the fridge.

(Fresh Kills, located 14 miles (22.5 kms) from Manhattan, absorbs 100,000 tonnes of garbage a week from New York, half the city's output. It is the world's largest landfill, holding some 2.4 billion

239

cubic feet (68m cu metres) of refuse – more than 25 times the volume of the Great Pyramid of Giza.)

By excavating people's bins, Professor Rathje and colleagues have also discovered that people buy less healthy food than they claim and that there are few truly healthy eaters.

Rathje, who used to dig up ancient Mayan burial mounds, was inspired to take up garbology by the activities of A.J. Weberman, who rifled through the dustbins of famous people like Bob Dylan, Henry Kissinger, Richard Nixon and others, drawing conclusions about their psychology and lifestyle from what he found there.

He denies that America will run out of space for landfills and drown in its own trash. He says, 'We will simply rise above it and live on the top.'

Ducia Atoll is one of the world's last untouched islands, situated 293 miles (470 kms) from Pitcairn island in the Pacific and 3,000 miles (5,000 kms) from the nearest continent. Zoologist Tim Benton visited it in 1991 to study the island's rare insect life and discovered on its beaches nearly one thousand items of junk during a 1¹/₂-mile (2.4-km) stroll along the shore.

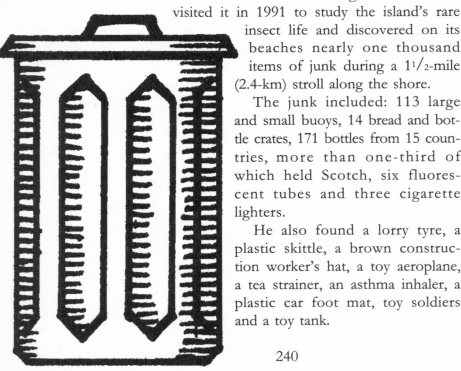

The junk included: 113 large and small buoys, 14 bread and bottle crates, 171 bottles from 15 countries, more than one-third of which held Scotch, six fluorescent tubes and three cigarette lighters.

He also found a lorry tyre, a plastic skittle, a brown construction worker's hat, a toy aeroplane, a tea strainer, an asthma inhaler, a plastic car foot mat, toy soldiers and a toy tank.

Nauru is the smallest and richest independent republic in the world. An island 8½ miles (13.6 kms) square, located midway between Melbourne and Honolulu, it is largely composed of one of the purest deposits of calcium phosphate in the world, which is exported and used as fertilizer.

In 1974, the Nauru Phosphate Corporation made $123 million profit on 1.9 million tonnes of phosphate – nearly $31,000 for every Nauruan citizen. By the time the phosphate runs out in 1995, careful investment will mean that each living Nauruan will be worth half a million dollars.

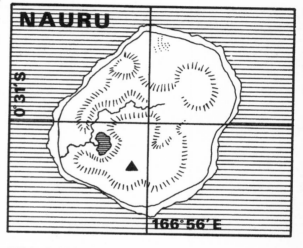

Nauru has its own airline with 44 pilots, a six-vessel shipping company and a $3.8 million hotel with a French chef. The island has one of the highest rates of car ownership in the world. With 2,000 cars, trucks and bikes on the island, there are a lot of accidents as a result. There is no income tax, and electricity is free. All the phosphate mining is done by an imported work force.

President Hammer De Roburt, a chain smoker who bears a physical resemblance to Edward G. Robinson, also designed the national flag.

The greens on the nine-hole golf course consist of coral sand. Players carry a small rake and are permitted to smooth the sand before putting.

Eighty years of mining have produced 60 million tonnes of phosphate but have devastated most of the island, leaving only a narrow coastal fringe on which the islanders live, in a parody of Western lifestyles.

241

When the *Queen Mary* was launched by her namesake in 1934, some 200,000 people lined the dockside to see the vast liner that had come to symbolize the national will to defeat the Depression. With a dead-weight of 81,237 tonnes, riveted steel sides nine storeys high and 4 acres (1.6 hectares) of teak decks, she was impressive on every level. For example, her propellers were the world's largest, each measuring more than 20 feet (6 metres) across and weighing 35 tonnes. However, they caused so much vibration in the ship's stern that, after a few voyages, they were quietly scrapped and replaced by propellers of an entirely different design.

She set sail on her maiden transatlantic voyage on 27 May 1936 carrying 2,000 passengers in great luxury. Two years later she won the Blue Riband for the fastest Atlantic crossing. During the war she became a troopship, ferrying troops to the European war zone at a top speed of 28.5 knots, enabling her to outrun U-boats. She was never hit but, in an incident hushed up until the war's end, she did run down her cruiser escort HMS *Curaçao* with the loss of more than 300 lives. The *Queen* suffered only a dented bow.

In 1967 when she was sold to Long Beach in California for $3.45 million and began a new life as 365-room hotel, she came complete with an undiscovered cache of wine and an 1828 harpsichord in the crew's quarters.

As part of a renovation job, 320 tonnes of paint were removed from the ship, causing her to rise a quarter of an inch (6 mm) higher in the water. The chips of paint removed from the ship contained traces of her wartime grey coating, and were sold for a handsome profit to nostalgia buffs by a local entrepreneur.

For many years she remained a prime tourist

attraction. Officially classified as a building and listed as a city department, the *Queen Mary* became one of Long Beach's biggest employers. She was used in many films, including *The Poseidon Adventure* and *Raise the Titanic*. One thousand brides a year pay to get married in her wedding chapel.

She was subsequently bought by the Walt Disney Company in 1988, which managed to lose $5 million or more on her every year – she is ruinously expensive to maintain – and her future was for a long time in doubt.

When she was first moored at Long Beach, a giant cavity 200 feet (61 metres) long and five decks tall was opened up inside her to provide exhibition space. This has weakened her structure, making it impossible to take her into the open sea without strengthening. The expense of moving her to a scrapyard capable of handling her – she is nearly three times the size of any other permanently preserved historical ship – would be far greater than the value of the scrap.

In December 1992, the city of Long Beach agreed to lease the ship to Joseph Prevratil, a Californian business consultant who administered the ship during the 1980s. She will stay where she is as a tourist attraction and hotel.

DURIAN

One of the most distinctive tropical fruits is the durian, whose creamy flesh and texture are suggestive of almonds, sherry, custard and ice cream. However it smells awful. One writer describes its odour as a 'mixture of old cheese and onions flavoured with

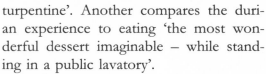

turpentine'. Another compares the durian experience to eating 'the most wonderful dessert imaginable – while standing in a public lavatory'.

The product of a large tree of the kapok family *(Durio zibethinus)*, the fruit, which can weigh up to 15 lbs (6.8 kgs), is enclosed in a spiky shell which makes harvesting it dangerous.

The ripe fruit is banned from many public places in Malaysia, Singapore, Thailand and Indonesia. It is recommended to eat the fruit outdoors, as the odour clings to walls, furnishings and clothing for days.

Durian eaters report that a warm feeling comes over them while devouring the fruit, which explains its reputation as an aphrodisiac.

TURING'S TREASURE

In 1940 Alan Turing, the mathematician and computer pioneer, became so worried about the possible effect of a German invasion of England on his bank balance that he invested all of his spare cash, about £250 ($355), in two silver bullion bars, wheeled them out into the woods in an old pram and buried them in the ground and in the bed of a stream. He wrote down instructions for retrieving the treasure and encoded them.

After the end of the war Turing and his friends made three attempts to locate the buried ingots, but all ended in failure, despite the use of a commercial metal detector as well as a model that he had designed himself.

They managed to find the old pram, but many of the landmarks on which his encoded instructions depended had changed – a bridge over the stream had been moved, and the bed of the stream had been concreted over.

When a friend asked why he hadn't made a map, Turing replied, 'Ah, that would have been bad security.'

QAT

Qat (rhymes with cot and sometimes spelled 'kat' or 'khat') is an evergreen shrub *(Catha edulis),* which is extensively cultivated high in the mountains in many Arab countries, especially the Yemen, for its narcotic leaf. The leaves, which are chewed to release their juice, contains amphetamine-related alkaloids, which provide stimulation comparable to several cups of coffee.

First brought from Ethiopia at least 600 years ago, qat is estimated to be worth $1 billion annually in North Yemen, a hundred times more than the value of all the nation's exports.

A national obsession, qat-chewing may consume as much as four hours of a day and one-third of a family's income. Chewing usually starts in the Yemen around 2 p.m. in a special relaxation room in the house known as the *mafraj.* A majority of Yemenites indulge in  this habit every day, which appears to do wonders for the national spirit but not a great deal for the economy. The farmers in the mountains have a sophisticated distribution network that brings the freshly-harvested young leaves to the eager consumers. For them the only disadvantage is that it turns your teeth green.

During the early years of the Second World War, German U-boats were sinking thousands of tonnes of Allied shipping every month, ten times as fast as they could be built. The best defence would have been aircraft patrols, but aircraft then had limited flying ranges and were unable to refuel in mid-air, so air cover was limited to within a few hundred miles of the coast.

In 1942, the English inventor Geoffrey Pyke put forward a solution – a giant floating mid-Atlantic airstrip made of ice. This ice-ship, more than 20 times the size of the *Queen Elizabeth*, would have been 300 feet (90 metres) wide and 2,000 feet (610 metres) long and consisted of a hollow ice-hull, with a landing strip on top and hangars, workshops, crew quarters and a refrigeration plant below. It would have had walls 30 feet (9 metres) thick and displaced 1.8 million tonnes of water.

Such a ship could not only have carried 200 Spitfires and 100 Mosquito bombers, but also, on a single voyage, all the food, raw materials and equipment required by Britain in a year, thus replacing the vulnerable merchant ship fleet.

It received the enthusiastic support of Winston Churchill, and was named HMS *Habakkuk* after the Old Testament prophet who said, 'I will work a work in your days, which ye will not believe, though it be told you.'

Secret research was begun and a 60-foot (18-metre) model was constructed on Patricia Lake, Alberta, using Pykrete (Pyke's concrete), a mixture of ice with up to 14 per cent sawdust. It had a crush resistance of 3,000 lbs per square inch, proved to be more stable than ice at high temperatures and, because it had a specific gravity lower than that of ice, was unsinkable. Bombs and torpedoes fired at it also proved it to be unmeltable and unsplinterable.

It was estimated that it would take 8,000 men eight months to freeze and assemble the 280,000 Pykrete blocks required for the full-scale ship, at an estimated cost of $70 million – at least as much as a conventional aircraft carrier – and the project was abandoned.

LONDON SIGNS

There were no street numbers in London until the latter part of the eighteenth century, as few people could read or write. Before that shops, taverns and commercial premises were identified by signboards, providing a forest of colourful images. These hanging signs employed several basic symbols: a beaver for hatters, a pineapple for confectioners, an olive tree for oilmen, a Bible for booksellers, a golden fleece for woollen-drapers, a rainbow for dyers, a peacock for gold-lacemen and so on.

But this shorthand soon began to break down. Some devices were used by many different trades, while others appeared in puzzling amalgamations, such as a chemist who traded under a sign of a civet cat and three herrings. Ambitious and spectacular signs could be specially commissioned at a cost of 100 guineas from one of the coach- and sedan-chair painters in Long Acre.

The bewildering volume of signs, coupled with the danger they posed (one enormous sign in Bridge Lane fell down, pulling the front of the house with it and killing four people) and the need to simplify directions and addresses, spelt an end to the days of the sign. In 1762 and 1764 signs were abolished in Westminster and the City, and the numbering of houses was adopted in 1768.

ORIGAMI

Origami, the art of paper-folding, was first invented in China and developed to a fine art in Japan. According to Michael Shall (who may be the only professional paper-folder in the Western Hemisphere), 'Paper-folding wasn't limited to the East. It sprang up independently all over the world . . . Samuel Johnson folded paper. Leonardo da Vinci folded paper. Lewis Carroll folded paper. Houdini folded paper. People were folding paper in Spain during the Inquisition. Wherever there is paper you'll find people folding it.'

In 1983 the American Museum of Natural History exhibited a Christmas tree covered and surrounded by 3,000 origami animals and plants, several origami dioramas and a vast mobile of origami stars.

Origami's foremost maestro was Akira Yoshizawa who, in 1937, at the age of 26, devoted himself to his art. He never sold any of his creations and more than 20,000 of them were kept carefully packed away in his home. His most difficult subject was the cicada – it took him 23 years to get it right.

Glaswegian artist/philosopher George Wylie created a paper boat, the *Origami*, which was launched on the Clyde on 6 May 1989 during the city's Mayfest. It was 60 feet long and 40 feet wide (18 x 12 metres).

A new folding style called 'box pleating' was introduced into origami in the 1960s and resulted in some of the most fantastic paper structures yet produced. They included Neal Elias's 'Llopio's Moment of Truth', in which a bull, a bullfighter and his cape are all folded from a single sheet of paper, and Robert Lang's 'Black Forest Cuckoo Clock', which contains 61 feet (20 metres) of creases in a model 16 inches (40 cms) high and takes four to six hours to fold.

VOLKSWAGEN

The *Volkswagen* (German for 'people's car') was designed in the 1930s by Dr Ferdinand Porsche and commissioned by Hitler who, it is said, suggested that the car looked like a beetle. Hitler subsequently laid the foundation stone of the first Volkswagen factory at Wolfsburg in 1938; more than 300,000 Germans invested in a hire-purchase plan for the car, buying stamps to stick in a book, which when complete entitled them to one blue/grey 'Beetle', the only colour available. Ironically, this symbol of Nazi propaganda never went into mass-production until the plant was taken over by the British Army – who became the first big customer by ordering 20,000 of them.

Since then its reliability has become legendary. Unmodified Beetles were used in the Antarctic in sub-zero conditions. A Beetle half-buried in the Libyan desert for five months started again at the first try; another, fitted with a propeller, crossed the Straits of Messina to Sicily in 38 minutes – two minutes faster than the ferry service. In the United States, a 'Babies Born in Beetles Club' has over 50 members.

Production of the Beetle ended in Germany in 1978 but it is still being manufactured in Mexico. The plant there made the 21 millionth Volkswagen in September 1992, a record number for a single model.

TEAZLE

Fuller's teazle is probably the only field-grown plant still used in its pure form in industrial processing. Because the seed heads of the thistly teazle are covered with sharp hooks, they are used to brush knitted garments and raise the pile on woven cloths. Mohair and cashmere get the teazle treatment, as does the green baize on snooker tables.

The last teazle merchant in Britain is the firm of Edmund Taylor in Huddersfield, which handles eight million teazles a year. Their business is threatened because of the shortage of growers.

There was once a heavy trade in teazles between Somerset, where the plant has been grown for 700 years, and the northern textile industry.

TESTICLE TRANSPLANT

The world's first testicle transplant was performed in St Louis, Missouri, in 1977, when surgeons transferred one testicle from one twin (who had two) to his identical twin (who had none).

The successful operation enabled both to produce fertile sperm. Surgeons said the operation was feasible only for identical twins, and then only where one has no testicles at all.

DISASTER-STAGER

W. Bruce Smith earned his living by staging disasters in dramatic plays. Among his most famous scenes were floods, shipwrecks, and the chariot race in the stage version of *Ben-Hur*.

He once staged a 'sandstorm' using ground-up cork. It worked until someone opened a door backstage and the 'sand' was blown over the first eight rows in the Drury Lane Theatre, London. He died at the age of 90 – during a fit of laughter.

SUICIDE

Some 50 years ago, Raymond Bloch – who was wanted by the police in an assault case – used four methods to end his life at the Belvedere Hotel in New York. To ensure success, he slashed his wrists with a razor blade, drank a bottle of disinfectant, attempted to strangle himself with a handkerchief, and then slipped below the surface of a bathtub full of water. He made it.

In 1987 the French National Assembly passed a bill to punish 'incitement to suicide', which carries a maximum prison sentence of three years and a fine of 200,000 francs ($36,000). This was in response to the publication of a book called *Suicide, Mode d'Emploi* by Claude Guillon and Yves le Bonniec, which sold 120,000 copies between 1982 and 1987.

The suicide rate in America increased by some 12 per cent following the death of Marilyn Monroe.

On 2 April 1976, a young man committed suicide in Paris by causing a piano to crush his skull as he lay on a bed. The piano had been balanced precariously against a plank.

In May 1983, an unemployed labourer from Newark, Nottinghamshire, killed himself by hammering two 5-inch (13-cm) nails into his head.

In May 1987, a retired carpenter from Sussex killed himself by drilling a hole in his heart with an electric drill because he couldn't stand the pain from angina pectoris, a heart condition.

251

The word 'hooligan' entered the language after the Bank Holiday disturbances of 1898, but there are many different versions of its origin.

Clarence Rook in his book *The Hooligan Nights* claims it originated with one Patrick Hooligan, an Irishman who lived in London's Elephant and Castle, earned his living as a bouncer and died in prison after killing a policeman.

Other possible sources are a character in the comic *Nuggets*, a music-hall act called the 'The Hooligans', and the American word 'hoodlum'. Yet another story was that at the trial of two prize-fighter brothers called Hoolehan, a policeman mis-pronounced their name.

The truth is that a Mr Edward Terah Hooley was on trial in 1898 after a corruption scandal involving the payment of 'slush money' to bike manufacturers had been uncovered. Hooley achieved notoriety by implicating many famous names, and jokes like 'Hooleybaloo' and 'Hooleyism' filled the popular press. After this many gangs started calling themselves 'hooligans', and the word passed into the language.

Hooliganism associated with sport can be traced back to the rivalry between chariot-racing fans of ancient Rome, who supported the drivers dressed in white, red, blue or green. Blues and greens were particularly vicious rivals, and in Constantinople these factions allied themselves with political groups. The Emperor Justinian's full-blooded support of the blues resulted in a riot in which many greens were slaughtered and the centre of the city was almost destroyed by fire. As a result, races were banned for five years.

MALAGASY

Formerly known as Madagascar, the Republic of Malagasy is the fourth largest island in the world and sole habitat of the lemurs, a unique race of primates.

Its first effective king was Andrianampoinimelina. His son, Radama I, died accidentally in a drunken fit in 1828 and his widow – Queen Ranavalona the Terrible – took power. For 33 years she ran a repressive regime during which an estimated one million of her subjects died or were executed while she lived in European-style luxury.

Her huge wooden palace was built in 1839 by Jean Laborde, who had been shipwrecked and landed naked on the island's eastern shore. A resourceful Frenchman who could turn his hand to any scientific or mechanical problem, he became the queen's confidant and mentor.

Using slave labour he also constructed an entire industrial town for 10,000 workers, which contained a silk plant, a paper mill, a cement factory, a sugar refinery and a cannon factory.

Malagasy, which is the size of France and has more than ten million inhabitants, is now one of the most heavily eroded places on Earth, as it has been stripped of 90 per cent of its forests.

WORLD-WIDE WORMS

Jim Wolfe, a former restaurateur of Des Plaines, Illinois, runs World-Wide Worms, a company that raises worms for fish bait, fertilizer and research purposes. He has also collected some 75 recipes for a 'cooking with worms' book, which include such delights as worms à la chocolate mousse and Caesar salad with worm croutons. Wolfe himself eats 1 lb (0.4 kgs) of worms a week and sprinkles worm chips on his breakfast cereal.

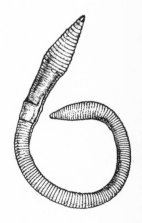

BOOKS:

A.S. E. Ackerman, *Popular Fallacies*
   (Old Westminster Press 1950)

William Amos, *The Originals: Who's Really Who in Fiction*
   (Sphere Books 1985)

William Arens, *The Man-Eating Myth*
   (Oxford University Press 1979)

Don Atyeo, *Blood & Guts: Violence In Sports*
   (Paddington Press 1979)

Ronald H. Bailey, *Glacier* (Time-Life 1982)

Thomas A. Bass, *The Newtonian Casino* (Longman 1990)

The Bathroom Readers' Institute, *Uncle John's Third
   Bathroom Reader* (St Martin's Press 1990)

Brent Berlin & Paul Kay, *Basic Color Terms: Their
   Universality and Evolution* (University of California
   Press 1992)

John Blackwood, *London's Immortals: the Complete
   Outdoor Commemorative Statues* (Savoy Press 1989)

Kenneth Boulding, *The Image* (Ann Arbor 1961)

Richard Brautigan, *The Abortion: A Historical Romance 1966*
   (Touchstone 1970)

A. W. Brian, *Cannibalism and the Common Law*
   (Chicago University Press 1984)

John G. Burke, *Cosmic Debris: Meteorites In History*
   (University of California Press 1986)

Hadley Cantril, *The Invasion from Mars*
   (Princeton University Press 1983)

James W. Clarke, *American Assassins*
   (Princeton University Press 1990)

Cocoa: The Story of its Cultivation
   (Cadbury Brothers Ltd 1927)

Basil Collier, *The Airship* (Hart-Davis, MacGibbon 1974)

Barnaby Conrad III, *Absinthe: History In A Bottle*
   (Chronicle Books 1988)

William R. Corliss, *Handbook of Unusual Natural Phenomena*
   (The Sourcebook Project, Glen Arm, Maryland 1977)

J. Y. Cousteau, *The Silent World* (The Reprint Society 1954)

Tom Crouch, *The Bishop's Boys: A Life of Wilbur and
   Orville Wright* (W.W. Norton 1991)

Andy Crump, *Dictionary of Environment and Development*
   (Earthscan 1991)

Tom Dardis, Keaton: *The Man Who Wouldn't Lie Down*
  (Penguin 1980)
David Day, *The Doomsday Book of Animals* (Ebury Press 1981)
A. F. L. Deeson, *An Illustrated History of Airships*
  (Spurbooks Ltd 1973)
The Diagram Group, *The Book of Comparisons*
  (Sidgwick & Jackson 1980)
Did You Know? (Reader's Digest 1990)
Robert T. Dodd, *Thunderstones and Shooting Stars*
  (Harvard University Press 1986)
Penelope Reed Doob, *The Idea of the Labyrinth from Classical
  Antiquity through the Middle Ages* (Cornell University
  Press 1990)
Edward Jay Epstein, *The Diamond Invention* (Hutchinson 1982)
Facts & Fallacies (Reader's Digest 1988)
Adrian Fisher & George Gerster, *The Art of the Maze*
  (Weidenfeld & Nicolson 1990)
Mike Fox and Richard James, *The Complete Chess Addict*
  (Faber & Faber 1987)
John Foster Fraser, *Round The World On a Wheel*
  (Chatto & Windus 1899/1982)
Michel Gauquelin, *The Cosmic Clocks* (Paladin 1973)
Daniel Gerould, *Guillotine: Its Legend and Lore* (Blast 1992)
Fred Gettings, *The Hand* (Paul Hamlyn 1965)
Jonathan Goldman, *The Empire State Building Book*
  (St Martin's Press 1987)
Nigel Gosling, *Gustave Doré* (David & Charles 1973)
Peter Gould & Rodney White, *Mental Maps* (Penguin 1974)
R. L. Gregory, *Eye and Brain* (Weidenfeld & Nicolson 1966)
Tim Halliday, *Vanishing Birds* (Penguin 1980)
Sir Ambrose Heal, *The Signboards of Old London Shops*
  (Batsford 1980)
Kenneth Heuer, *Thunder, Singing Sands and Other Wonders*
  (Dodd Mead 1981)
High Times Encyclopedia of Recreational Drugs (Stonehill
  Publishing 1978)
Christopher Hill, Barry Reay & William Lamont, *The World
  of the Muggletonians* (Temple Smith 1983)
Andrew Hodges, *Alan Turing: the Enigma* (Burnett Books 1983)
Banesh Hoffmann, *Albert Einstein* (Paladin 1977)
Ian Hogbin, *The Island of Menstruating Men* (Chandler Publishing
  Co., Toronto 1970)

SOURCES

Bert Hölldobler & Edward O. Wilson, *The Ants*
(Harvard University Press 1990)

James D. Horan & Paul Sann, *Pictorial History of the Wild West*
(Spring Books 1954)

Beryl Hugill, *Bring On The Clowns* (Chartwell Books Inc. 1980)

John M. Hull, *Touching The Rock: An Experience of Blindness*
(Pantheon 1991)

Peter L. Jakab, *Visions of a Flying Machine: The Wright Brothers and
the Process of Invention* (Smithsonian Institution Press 1990)

Susanna Johnston & Tim Beddow, *Collecting: The Passionate
Pastime* (Viking 1986)

Robert Jungk, *Tomorrow Is Already Here* (Rupert Hart-Davis 1954)

David Kempe, *Living Underground* (Herbert Press 1988)

Norman Kolpas, *The Chocolate Lover's Companion*
(Quick Fox 1979)

Egon Larsen, *Strange Sects & Cults* (Arthur Barker 1971)

David Levy & Monty Newborn, *How Computers Play Chess*
(W. H. Freeman 1990)

The Library of Curious and Unusual Facts (Time-Life 1990)

Harry McSween, Jr, *Meteorites and Their Parent Planets*
(Cambridge University Press 1987)

Adrianne Marcus, *The Chocolate Bible* (G. P. Putnam 1979)

Kathleen Mark, *Meteorite Craters* (University of Arizona
Press 1988)

Herbert Marshall (ed.), *The Battleship Potemkin* (Avon 1978)

Peter Matthiessen, *Baikal: Sacred Sea of Siberia*
(Thames & Hudson 1992)

William J. Mitchell, *Computer-Aided Architectural Design*
(Van Nostrand Reinhold 1977)

Greta Nilsson et al, *Facts About Furs* (Animal Welfare Institute,
Washington, DC 1980)

Oceanography: Readings from Scientific American
(W. H. Freeman 1971)

Jerry E. Patterson, *The City of New York*
(Harry N. Abrams Inc. 1978)

Geoffrey Pearson, *Hooligan* (Macmillan 1983)

Brian Pejovic, *Man and Meteorites* (Thames Head 1982)

Roger Tory Peterson, *The Birds* (Time-Life 1964)

Clive Ponting, *A Green History of the World* (Penguin 1992)

The Reader's Digest Book of Strange Stories/Amazing Facts
(Reader's Digest 1975)

The Real Cowboy (Barrie & Jenkins 1976)

Alistair Revie, Thomas Foster & Burton Graham, *Battle: A History of Conflict on Land, Sea and Air* (Enigma Books 1974)

Carol Anne Rinzler, *Chocolate* (Signet 1979)

Clarence Rook, *The Hooligan Nights* (Oxford University Press 1899/1979)

Witold Rybczynski, *Taming The Tiger* (Penguin 1983)

William Sargant, *The Mind Possessed* (Heinemann 1973)

Pedro Silmon, *The Bikini* (Virgin Books 1986)

Kenneth G. V. Smith, *A Manual of Forensic Entomology* (British Museum 1987)

David Spanier, *Total Chess* (Secker & Warburg 1984)

Ray Tannahill, *Flesh and Blood* (Hamish Hamilton 1974)

Mary Tich & Richard Findlater, *Little Tich: Giant of the Music Hall* (Elm Tree Books 1979)

William A. Tidwell et al, *Come Retribution: The Confederate Secret Service and the Assassination of Lincoln* (University Press of Mississippi 1988)

H. A. Tyler, *Pueblo Gods and Myths* (University of Oklahoma Press 1964)

Peter Verney, *Homo Tyrannicus* (Mills & Boon 1979)

Margaret Visser, *The Rituals of Dinner* (Viking 1992)

David Wallechinsky & Irving Wallace, *The People's Almanac 2* (Bantam Books. 1978)

David Wallechinsky & Irving Wallace, *The People's Almanac 3* (Bantam Books 1981)

Lyall Watson, *Lifetide* (Hodder & Stoughton 1979)

Arthur Weingarten, *The Sky Is Falling* (Grosset & Dunlap 1977)

Richard Westfall, *Never At Rest* (Cambridge University Press 1981)

Tim D. White, *Prehistoric Cannibalism* (Princeton University Press 1992)

Colin Wilson & Pat Pitman, *Encyclopedia of Murder* (Pan 1964)

Gerald L. Wood FZS, *The Guinness Book of Animal Facts & Feats* (Guinness Superlatives Ltd 1982)

Jennifer Woolfe, *The Potato in the Human Diet* (Cambridge University Press 1987)

John Robert Young, *The French Foreign Legion* (Thames & Hudson 1988)

SOURCES

MAGAZINES/NEWSPAPERS:

Arab Report & Memo
Architectural Design
Christian Science Monitor
Country Life
Crawdaddy
Daily Express
Daily Mail
Daily Mirror
Daily Telegraph
Discover
The Economist
Esquire
Evening Argus
Evening Standard
Financial Times
Guardian
Harper's & Queen
The Herbalist
Horizon
Iceberg Research
Illustrated London News
Independent
Independent on Sunday
International Herald Tribune
The Lady
The Lancet
The Listener
Look and Learn
Mail on Sunday
National Enquirer

National Geographic
Natural History
New Musical Express
New Scientist
Newsweek
New West
New Yorker
New York Times
Observer
Omni
Playboy
Publishers Weekly
Rolling Stone
Science '83
Science Digest
The Sciences
Scientific American
Soho Weekly News
South
Sunday Correspondent
Sunday Telegraph
Sunday Times
Time
Time Out
The Times
The Times Literary Supplement
US
Variety
Vegetarian Times
Warmer Bulletin

NOTE TO SOURCES

All the material in this book has been drawn from the published sources detailed on this and the preceding pages. In producing such a book, I have tried to combine good journalistic practice and common sense, working always from the best available and most reliable sources and paying strict attention to the conventions of copyright. Any inaccuracies that have found their way into the text are the responsibility of the author.

Strenuous efforts have been made to ensure that proper acknowledgment to sources has been given, but we will happily amend any omissions in future editions of the book.

Any readers with queries, corrections or additional Curious Facts may address them to the author, c/o Collins & Brown.

ACKNOWLEDGMENTS

It is my pleasure to be able to thank the people who have helped bring this book to fruition over the last two and a half years.

Firstly my thanks go to the designer of the book, Andy Gammon, who has handled a very complex job with great equanimity and who has, on this and many other projects, proved both his professionalism and his friendship.

Similar sentiments go to my colleague Ian Whitelaw, who was there during the long and tedious processes of editing and fact-checking. Thanks for seeing the book through some very dark nights with your cheeriness and your Berber songs.

To Tanya Seton I owe a great deal more than words can say. She has not only handled the copy typing of the manuscript with meticulous precision but has also shared the twenty years of my life since I began clipping papers. Love also to our sons Alex and Louis.

My thanks in addition to Nadine Seton, for stepping into the breach so efficiently, and to Raphael Whittle and Adam Throup, for all the work they put in,which was greatly appreciated. Thanks also to Alan Shelley of the Bow Windows bookshop in Lewes for supplying key volumes.

At my publisher's I would like to thank personally Mark Collins and Cameron Brown for their extreme patience over this long and complicated period; Roger Bristow; and especially Mandy Greenfield for being such a good editor and taking all the problems in her stride.

Special thanks to Kieran Fogarty (love to you, wherever you are) for making it happen and for all the other things that we never talked about.

Finally, this book grew out of two previously published books of unusual information. Many thanks to the original Curious Factors: Michael Marten, John Chesterman, John Trux, David Brittain and Lee Torrey. Gentlemen, the years have gone by but the strangeness remains.

JM

259

DEDICATION

To my mother/mum
Grace Kathleen May
with all my love
who first taught me
to be curious
and full of wonder
about the world
and
in memory
of her
childhood mentor and friend
Mr Salisbury
noted conchologist

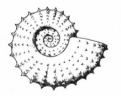